# Learn to
# make bead
# jewelry

# Learn to make bead jewelry

## WITH 35 FABULOUS PROJECTS

LYNN DAVY

KALMBACH BOOKS

A QUARTO BOOK

Learn to make bead jewelry with
35 fabulous projects

Copyright © 2016 Quarto Inc.

Kalmbach Books
21027 Crossroads Circle
Waukesha, Wisconsin 53186
www.Kalmbach.com/Books

First published in the United States in 2016 by
Kalmbach Books

Published in 2016
19 18 17 16 15   1 2 3 4 5

ISBN: 978-1-62700-284-4
EISBN: 978-1-62700-285-1

Conceived, designed, and produced by
Quarto Publishing plc, The Old Brewery,
6 Blundell Street, London N7 9BH

QUAR.FWSB

**Senior editor:** Katie Crous
**Designer:** Karin Skånberg
**Photographer:** Phil Wilkins
**Copy editor:** Claire Waite Brown
**Proofreader:** Liz Jones
**Art director:** Caroline Guest

**Creative director:** Moira Clinch
**Publisher:** Paul Carslake

Color separation in Singapore by
   Pica Digital Pte Ltd
Printed in China by Hung Hing Off-set
   printing Co Ltd

10 9 8 7 6 5 4 3 2 1
Library of Congress Control Number:
2015946884

# Contents

**Ocean**

Simple pleasures earrings
PAGE 28

**Beach**

Beach love beads
PAGE 38

**Meadow**

Wildflower wrap bracelet
PAGE 50

Pacific bracelet
PAGE 30

Talisman pendant
PAGE 32

Teardrop trio necklaces
PAGE 34

Wave pendant
PAGE 36

Jurassic Coast necklace
and earrings PAGE 40

Strandline bracelet
PAGE 44

Summer nights earrings
PAGE 46

Perfect pearl necklace
PAGE 48

Marigold bracelet
PAGE 52

Nostalgia necklace
PAGE 54

Sunny morning bracelet
PAGE 56

English garden necklace
PAGE 58

Continued next page

**Woodland**

Rustic romance bracelet
PAGE 60

**Forest**

Lilac lariat
PAGE 70

**Mountain**

Misty mountains collar
PAGE 82

**Volcano**

Volcanic vision necklace
PAGE 94

**Fall leaves necklace**
PAGE 62

**Crystal cascade necklace**
PAGE 64

**Oval pendant**
PAGE 66

**Spring birch earrings**
PAGE 68

**Forest glade necklace**
PAGE 72

**Pear tree bracelet**
PAGE 76

**Cherry harvest earrings**
PAGE 78

**Charm cluster necklace**
PAGE 80

**Silk and stone bracelet**
PAGE 86

**Rugged rocks necklace**
PAGE 88

**True blue heart necklace**
PAGE 90

**Highland heather bracelet**
PAGE 92

**Dramatic dangle earrings**
PAGE 96

**Glowing treasures collar**
PAGE 98

**Drama queen necklace**
PAGE 102

**Light my fire necklace**
PAGE 106

Bead jewelry is fun and satisfying to make. Discover a world of design and color as you embark on your own beading adventure.

# Welcome to my world of beads

**Find your style**

Create your own unique style with the techniques you'll learn in this book. Most projects can be completed in an afternoon, and there are lots of clear photos and expert tips to help you.

In a wide world of bead stores—all packed with a dazzling variety of beads and components—where do you start?

Let me be your beady guide. In this book I've organized a personal tour for you, based around seven color themes inspired by natural landscapes. Along the way, you'll learn the skills to become confident in making beautiful, comfortable, well-finished jewelry that anyone would be proud to wear.

In general, the simpler patterns are at the start (in the primeval ocean) and the more complex, statement pieces are later (as you climb through the mountains to the peak of the volcano). However, you don't have to take a linear trip: the book is designed so that you can jump in wherever you like.

You don't have to follow the patterns to the letter, either. My hope is that you'll use the projects as a starting point for your own personal journey of beady discovery—that you'll be inspired to ask "What if...?" and that you'll adapt, improve, and personalize these designs to make them truly your own. The most important element in your jewelry isn't the beads or the technique or the color scheme. It's you.

Now head down to your local bead store and see where the journey takes you. I hope you'll have as much fun as I did!

Lynn Davy

# About this book

Each project is self-contained and clearly set out with all the information you need to get started. See the design grow on the page, and watch your own creation grow alongside it. Here are some of the main features.

**Techniques** Essential beading skills, presented in simple steps and cross-referenced from the projects that use them.

**Close-ups** Important details are enlarged so that you can see them clearly.

**You will need** Complete lists of all beads, findings, and tools needed for each project.

**Tip** Handy hints and expert know-how to help you get the most out of a project.

**Finished size** Length and/or width as appropriate, given in both inches and centimeters.

**Technique** Step-by-step explanation of a key element or essential skill.

## Chapter 1
# Materials, tools, techniques

Here are the basics you'll need to get started making bead jewelry. Learn to recognize some different bead types; find out what tools you need; get acquainted with wires, threads, and jewelry findings. Along with advice on designing and some tips for effective bead shopping, you'll also find some of the most useful techniques placed here for easy reference.

# Beads, beads, beads

Walking into a bead store for the first time can be overwhelming. There are so many beautiful beads to choose from, and so many technical terms used to describe them, but what do they all mean? In the next few pages you'll learn how to recognize some of the different bead types so that you can start to make the right choices for your beading projects.

There are five things you need to consider when choosing a bead: color, finish, size, shape, and material. You might also want to know, for example, where it comes from, who made it, how it was made, whether it's fairly traded or environmentally sustainable, how old it is, whether it might cause allergies, whether it's colorfast, and, of course, how much it costs. These are all questions to ask your bead supplier or to research online.

## Color

There are many books you can turn to to learn more about color theory and color mixing. To begin, you can classify colors as warm, cold, or neutral. In the project palettes below, for example, Volcano is warm, Ocean is cold, and

Beach is neutral. When describing beads the opacity of the color is also important, especially for glass beads. Can you see through the bead, or not?

## Finish

Finish is closely related to color and refers to the outer surface of the bead. The surface may be matte, or it may have a "Picasso" coating (see page 101) or a rainbow iris or "Aurora Borealis" effect, commonly shortened to "AB." Half-coated beads have a metallic finish on one side only. A finish may modify the way the color appears, or it may allow some or all of the bead color to come through.

**PROJECT COLORS BY CHAPTER**

Each chapter of projects has its own nature-inspired color palette.

**Ocean** Cool, soothing blues and aquamarines, with sparkling pearls and silver

**Beach** Soft, neutral creams and sandy browns

**Meadow** Fresh, pretty florals, bright greens, and golden yellow

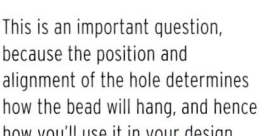

## WHERE'S THE HOLE?

This is an important question, because the position and alignment of the hole determines how the bead will hang, and hence how you'll use it in your design.

Some bead shapes are similar but the hole positions may be very different. And look at where the string goes.

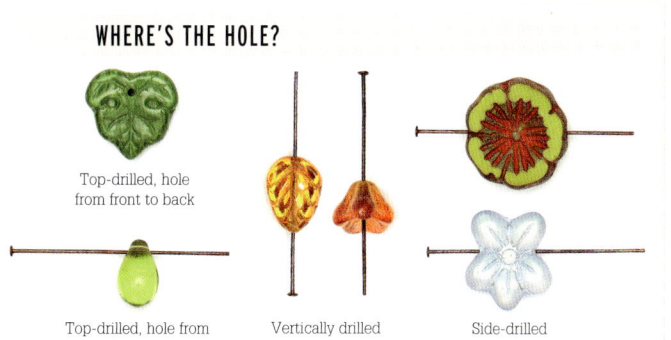

Top-drilled, hole from front to back

Top-drilled, hole from side to side

Vertically drilled

Side-drilled

### Seed bead sizes

15º =1.5mm

11º = 2.2mm

8º = 3mm

6º = 3.7mm

### Seed bead sizes

These are the most useful sizes for stringing projects. Note that seed bead sizes are odd: the bigger the number, the smaller the bead.

### Bead sizes

4mm

6mm

8mm

10mm

12mm

14mm

16mm

## Size

Beads can be found in all sizes, from tiny beads like grains of sand, to huge ones that can be worn on their own as a pendant. Note that bead sizes are usually given in millimeters (mm) at the bead store; there are just over 25mm to the inch. So a 25mm bead is approximately 1" in diameter, or, if you string 50 2mm beads you'll have a string about 4" long.

## Shape

There are probably hundreds of different bead shapes. Possibly more. The "Bead diversity" chart on page 14 shows you some of the amazing variety you can choose from; you'll find more in the individual projects.

## Material

Glass is by far the more common material for beadmaking, and it comes in many varieties, as you will see from the "Bead diversity" chart. There are many other options such as semiprecious stone, freshwater pearls, metal, polymer clay, or ceramic. As you work through the projects in this book, you'll learn about some different materials and how they influence your design choices.

**Woodland** Russet browns and bronze with a hint of bright green

**Forest** Lush, rich greens with berry red and deep purple

**Mountain** Stony grays and misty blues with metallic accents

**Volcano** Hot, glowing orange and dramatic reds

## BEAD DIVERSITY

The vast variety of beads available certainly provides the spice for your beading projects. The elements described on the previous pages—color, finish, size, shape, and material—all come into play and should be well considered before choosing the right beads for your project.

Copper hollow "stardust" rounds

Landscape jasper coin beads

Handmade polymer clay lentil

Lampwork glass saucer, opaque, decorated with stringer work

Czech pressed glass disks, center-drilled, transparent matte

Tumbled seaglass beads

Czech pressed glass daggers, matte AB

Bali-style silver rounds

Lampwork glass oval focal with encased flower decoration

Lampwork glass tab focal, opaque, with floral decoration

Firepolished faceted rounds, two-tone transparent

Firepolished faceted rounds, transparent

Czech pressed glass top-drilled leaves, matte transparent, half-coated AB

## Tip You get what you pay for

Try to buy lampwork beads from an artisan, and at the very least make sure the beads have been annealed (cooled under controlled conditions in a kiln) to avoid problems with cracking. Lampwork beads should have smooth, even holes without sharp edges, and the holes should be clean and free from dust or clay residue. If there is residue in the holes, remove carefully under water and avoid breathing it in, because the dust can cause lung problems.

Lampwork glass lentils with dots and gold foil

Semiprecious amazonite nugget beads

Lampwork flattened heart

Czech pressed glass druk (round) beads

Lampwork glass lentil, encased

Semiprecious malachite stone chips

Czech pressed glass leaves, opaque, vertically drilled

Japanese seed beads, matte transparent

Czech pressed glass faceted rondelles, opaque two-tone

Czech pressed glass flower beads, opaque with partial Picasso finish

Lampwork glass focal, transparent, with twisted core and dichroic glass

Japanese seed beads, transparent AB

Lampwork glass tube focal, opaque with raised decoration

Austrian crystal bicones and hearts, transparent

Copper-plated pewter spacer beads with Bali-style decoration

Firepolished faceted rounds, transparent

Semiprecious amazonite oblong pillows

Lampwork glass disk bead, matte

Chinese ceramic heart beads, handpainted

Lampwork glass round with frit (crushed glass) decoration

Polymer clay center-drilled disks

Japanese seed beads, matte transparent silver-lined

Freshwater pearls, natural gray

Hollow metal beads with Bali-style decoration

Red jade donut focal, hand-carved

Lampwork glass spacers, matte transparent

Freshwater pearls, dyed in various colors

Murano glass heart, silver-lined

Polymer clay bird focal, handmade, antique finish

Czech pressed glass pear bead, hand-painted

Abalone shell coin beads

Czech pressed glass Celtic-style beads, transparent, half-coated with metallic AB finish

## Tip Balancing act

Too much shine is hard on the eyes, while a predominance of matte finishes may cause some colors to disappear into the background. Try to mix up your colors and finishes to make your design stand out. You'll find lots of ideas for how to do this as you look through the projects that follow.

# What if you can't find that exact bead?

Some of the beads you'll see in this book's projects are handmade and unique. If you're on a tight budget, certain beads may be out of your reach. But don't worry, you can almost always substitute one bead for another and still get beautiful results.

For most of the projects it's the size—and to a lesser extent the shape—of the bead that's the most important factor. You can substitute beads that are a different material but the same diameter and still end up with a piece of jewelry of the same length. It may drape a little differently, since not all materials are the same weight, and you might need to choose a thicker stringing material if your beads have larger holes.

If you're substituting spherical beads for flat ones—for example in the Rustic romance bracelet on page 60—be aware that the internal diameter of your piece will be reduced, so you may need to add in an extra repeat or put more beads at the ends in order to keep the fit.

If you're substituting different shapes, take a good look at the alignment and placement of the holes (see Where's the hole?, page 13), since this will determine how the bead hangs in the finished piece.

## A FEW TIPS ON BEAD BUYING

**Be organized** Make a list and buy only what you need for the project you have in mind. Having said that, if you go to a bead fair or two, or find out when your local bead store or favorite online site is having a sale, you can pick up great bargains—just make sure you only buy beads you are likely to use, or your stash will be out of control before you know it.

**Try to buy in person** There is no substitute for handling and seeing beads "for real," and when buying in person you have the vendor on hand to answer your questions. You'll also gain a feel for the different materials and the quality of the beads on sale, and of course colors are much easier to see properly and match in daylight.

**Join an online forum or discussion group** Not only will you get great advice and support, these groups often have "swaps" or a section for "destash," where you can buy beads that other members have decided they're not going to use.

**There are alternatives to expensive materials** If you're still learning, or you're making things just for you and just for fun, you don't need to use Austrian crystal, or the finest gem-grade pearls, or 24kt gold. Instead you can find cheaper, sparkly crystal strands, freshwater pearls, and gold-plated beads that will give the same effect, at least from a distance. Save the expensive things for when you're confident in your techniques (after working through this book, you will be!) and you want to make something truly special and unique.

**Lampwork glass beads** are in a class of their own and are often quite expensive. The best ones are handmade by individual artists. Try to buy direct from the maker and ensure that the beads have been properly annealed (cooled under controlled conditions) to avoid problems with cracking. A good lampwork bead has a clean shape and smooth, even holes with no sharp edges. The holes should be clean and free from dust or clay residue. If you buy cheap lampwork beads with residue in the holes, remove it carefully with a bead reamer, preferably under water so you don't breathe in the dust, which can cause respiratory problems.

**Teardrop trio necklace, page 34**
The original design is three necklaces designed to be layered. This is a simplified version with different bead finishes and shapes.

Some of the teardrops are replaced by faceted rondelles to give a simpler outline.

Opaque Picasso drops are used in place of the transparent ones in the original.

Instead of a separate pendant, this version has the focal on the same necklace, suspended from a simple bail. In place of the lampwork heart, the focal is a drop-shaped bead in faux turquoise.

These peardrops are the same shape as the ones in the original, but a different color and finish for a more rustic look.

**Glowing treasures necklace, page 98**
A cool turquoise color scheme is just as pretty as the original bright red. Asymmetry isn't for everyone, so this version is a balanced composition with matching pairs of dangles, a central pendant, and the clasp at the back.

**Lilac lariat, page 70**
A lariat design is ideal for using whatever beads are in your stash. Start with a pair of focal beads for the ends of the lariat, and build a palette of colors around them.

## COLOR GRADIENTS

Lighter shades inside darker ones make the piece appear to glow. Choose your colors carefully as some will work better than others. Cobalt, sapphire, and turquoise blues make a nice gradient, but make sure the turquoise is not too green. Or try grading from pale pink through deeper rose to purple, or a white, gray, black monochrome transition. Matte transparent beads will give you less intense colors and hence a more subtle effect. And of course there is always the classic rainbow...

Turquoise and aqua glass pearls replace the red glass druks.

Four lampwork rounds are used instead of three, so the necklace is symmetrical.

Turquoise and ivory is a classic lampwork glass color combination. The focal is placed centrally on the necklace.

Reds, pinks, greens, and browns all complement or tone with the multicolored glass in the focal beads.

Flattened shapes are good for lariat ends. These hand-formed ovals are similar but not identical to each other.

Using copper in place of silver changes the whole look of the piece, as well as being more economical.

The focals are strung on eyepins and embellished with tassels of wrapped-loop dangles (see page 24).

Cool blues and stylish monochrome—just two of the beautiful color gradients waiting to be discovered.

C-Lon nylon cord

Waxed linen thread

Nylon beading threads

Flexible beading wire

Leather cord

NATURAL SILK
100% Naturseide

NATURAL SILK No. 10
100% Naturseide Ø 0,90 mm

www.griffin.de
For stringing
pearls and beads

www.griffin.de
For stringing
pearls and beads

Pearl stringing silk

# Stringing materials

This category broadly covers all the thin, flexible materials you put through your bead holes to string the beads together.

**Flexible beading wire** The stringing material most commonly used in this book, flexible beading wire consists of several strands of steel wire encased in plastic. Tough, flexible, and nonstretch, it should be trimmed with diagonal wire cutters (not scissors). Most of the projects in the book call for the "standard" seven-strand 0.018" (.46mm) diameter, but be aware that there are many different thicknesses available, so always read the label. There are also many different-colored finishes to choose from, so if you're making a project with exposed wire, such as the Crystal cascade necklace on page 64, choose a cable color or metallic finish that really complements your beads.

To finish off a design strung on flexible beading wire you will need crimps (see page 19) and crimping pliers (see page 21), and one of a choice of crimping techniques (see page 22).

**Braided beading thread** This tough, nonstretch nylon thread is also sold as fishing line. The 4lb (1.8kg) breaking strength is good for stitching small beads, but for stringing larger beads choose a higher breaking strength. This thread is more supple than flexible beading wire, but more prone to fraying, and is finished off with knots, not crimps.

**Nylon beading thread** There are many different brands of this thread, such as Nymo and K.O., mostly used for stringing and stitching the smallest beads. Nylon beading thread is not suitable for stringing heavy beads because it will stretch and fray, but it is good for stitching a delicate fringe or tassel to finish off a strung project (see Forest glade necklace, page 72).

**Silk** Stringing silk is prethreaded with a needle and is available in various thicknesses. It is particularly useful for stringing pearls (see page 48).

**Rattail/satin cord** This thick, shiny cord is good for stringing large-holed beads and pendants, and for decorative knotting.

**Cord and lace** Cord can be made of leather, waxed linen, hemp, nylon, or cotton. A lace is a thin strip of leather, suede, or faux suede that is good for stringing pendants. Both lace and cord may be finished with cord end crimps or ribbon end crimps (see page 33) so that metal clasps or findings can be attached.

**Ribbon** Pretty ribbons of silk, organza, or satin can be used to make an easy, instant pendant necklace. Finish with ribbon end crimps (see page 33) or a simple knotted slider clasp (see Wave pendant, page 36).

K.O. brand nylon beading thread

Faux suede lace

Hand-dyed silk ribbon

Rattail satin cord

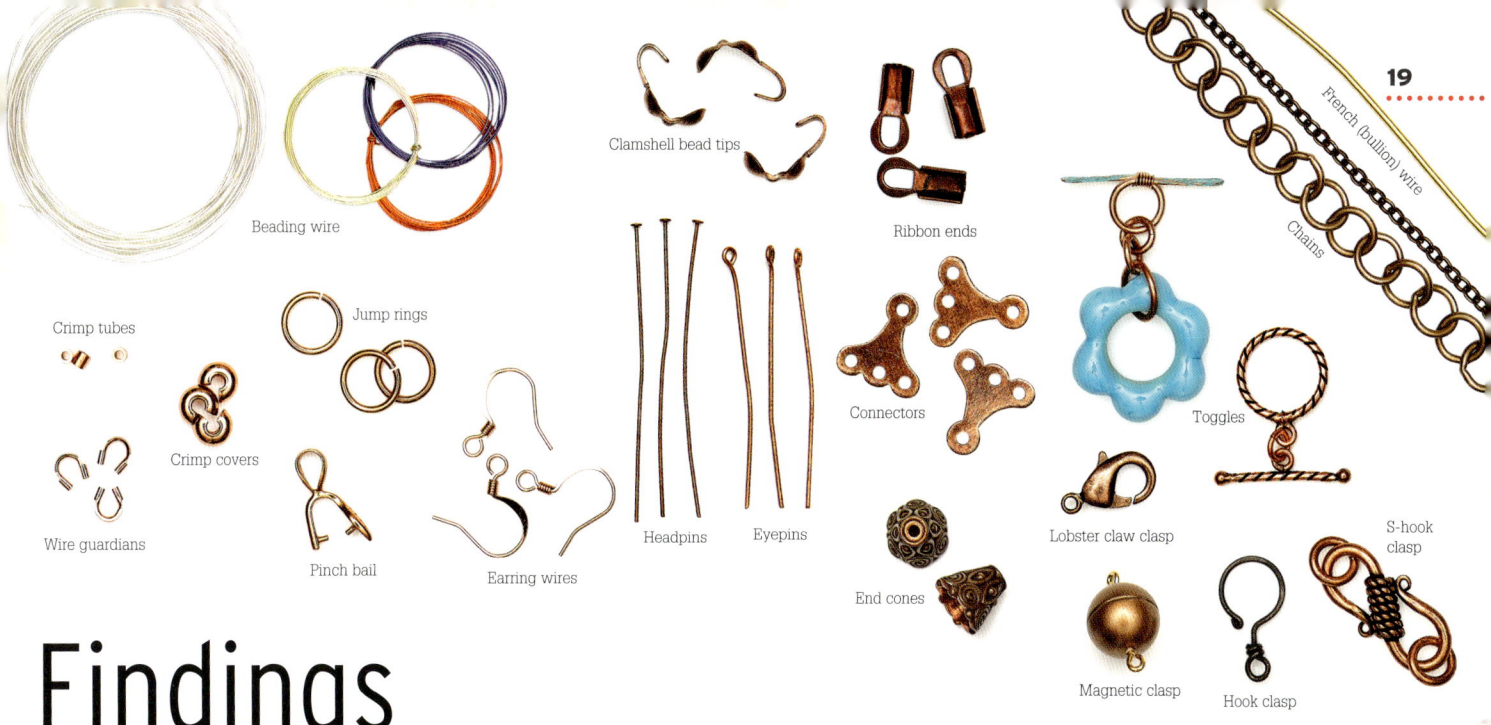

Beading wire

Clamshell bead tips

Ribbon ends

French (bullion) wire

Chains

Crimp tubes

Jump rings

Crimp covers

Connectors

Toggles

Wire guardians

Pinch bail

Earring wires

Headpins

Eyepins

End cones

Lobster claw clasp

S-hook clasp

Magnetic clasp

Hook clasp

# Findings

The word "findings" refers to all those handy little bits and pieces that enable you to put a piece of jewelry together. Mostly made of metal, they are worth getting to know because the right finding makes a designer's life so much easier!

Many of the projects in this book use copper findings. Copper is inexpensive, so if learning a new technique, always start and practice with copper. When you have built up your confidence you can move onto the more expensive metals, such as sterling silver.

**Wire** Wire makes up the basic material for many findings. After a while you may decide to buy raw wire and make your own.

**Headpins and eyepins** These are lengths of wire with a little disk or loop at the end to stop beads falling off the bottom. The most useful size is probably 2" (5cm), which is long enough for most of the dangles you'll find in this book.

**Earring wires** When making earrings, be aware of potential allergies, since some people cannot wear particular metals. Sterling silver is safe for most, but there are other hypoallergenic alternatives.

**Chain** Useful for decorative detailing as well as providing a base for charm bracelets or as a delicate necklace for a tiny pendant. Choose the metal, style, and size of chain according to your project.

**Jump rings** Most jump rings are "open," i.e., with the ends not joined, so the ring can be opened with pliers (see page 23) and used to join components together and to provide safety breakpoints. Most projects in this book call for either 4mm or 6mm jump rings. You can also obtain soldered or "fixed" rings with the ends permanently fused together, which are useful for making a secure connection.

**Bail** A component for suspending a pendant or bead. Pinch bails clip into the top of a pendant that is drilled from front to back and are ideal for crystal pendants.

**Crimps** Essential for finishing off many of the projects in this book, crimps are little metal tubes that can be squashed to hold the ends of beading wire securely. The most useful size is 2 x 2mm. See page 21 for crimping pliers and page 22 for techniques.

**Crimp covers** These hollow metal rounds can be used to cover your crimps—not just because your crimping technique isn't perfect yet, but also to change the appearance of your crimps if, say, you've used silver crimps in a copper necklace.

**Clamshell bead tips (calotte crimps)** Use with soft threads that are finished by knotting. See Perfect pearl necklace on page 48.

**Wire guardians** Tiny horseshoe-shapes that protect the ends of crimped wires and give a neat finish.

**French (bullion) wire** Coils of very fine wire, used to protect thread in traditionally strung pearls and gemstones (see page 54).

**Ribbon end crimps** Metal clamps that are fixed to the ends of ribbon or lace so a clasp can be attached. See page 33.

**End cones** Conical metal (occasionally glass) beads that fit over the ends of multiple strands.

**Connectors (links)** Usually metal, may have the same or a different number of holes at each end.

**Clasps** Toggle clasps are good for bracelets because they can be fastened one-handed. Lobster claw clasps are better for necklaces because they are spring-loaded and more secure.

**Bead reamer** A narrow, cylindrical metal file with a pointed tip. Use for cleaning and/or widening bead holes.

**Scissors** Use scissors to cut thread, fabric, and paper, but not wire, which will blunt or damage the scissors. The sharper the better.

# Toolbox

There are many, many tools available for jewelry making, and although they will undeniably make your creative life easier, thankfully you don't have to buy them all. Detailed here are all the tools you need to complete the projects in this book.

You can start with cheap, "beginner," tools, but you'll get better results if you buy the best you can afford—they'll last longer and be easier on your hands. Try some out if you can, to find which are most comfortable for you. This is particularly important if you're going to be doing a lot of wirework.

**Bead spinner** A bead spinner and its special curved needle (below) enable you to string tiny beads quickly and efficiently. See page 23.

**Bead scoop** For picking up small quantities of small beads. If you don't have one, use a teaspoon.

**Glue** Rarely necessary, but can be useful for stabilizing knots. Use a jeweler's glue, such as E-6000, or a two-part epoxy. Never use nail polish!

**Ruler** An essential tool. This one has a handy bead size guide as well as both inches and centimeters.

**BeadsRuleR.com**

| Bead sizes in millimeters | 2 | 3 | 4 | 5 | 6 | 7 | 8 | 9 | 10 | 12 | 14 | 16 | 18 | 20 |
|---|---|---|---|---|---|---|---|---|---|---|---|---|---|---|
| Approx # of beads/inch | 12.5 | 8.25 | 6.25 | 5.12 | 4.25 | 3.56 | 3.12 | 2.81 | 2.5 | | | | | |

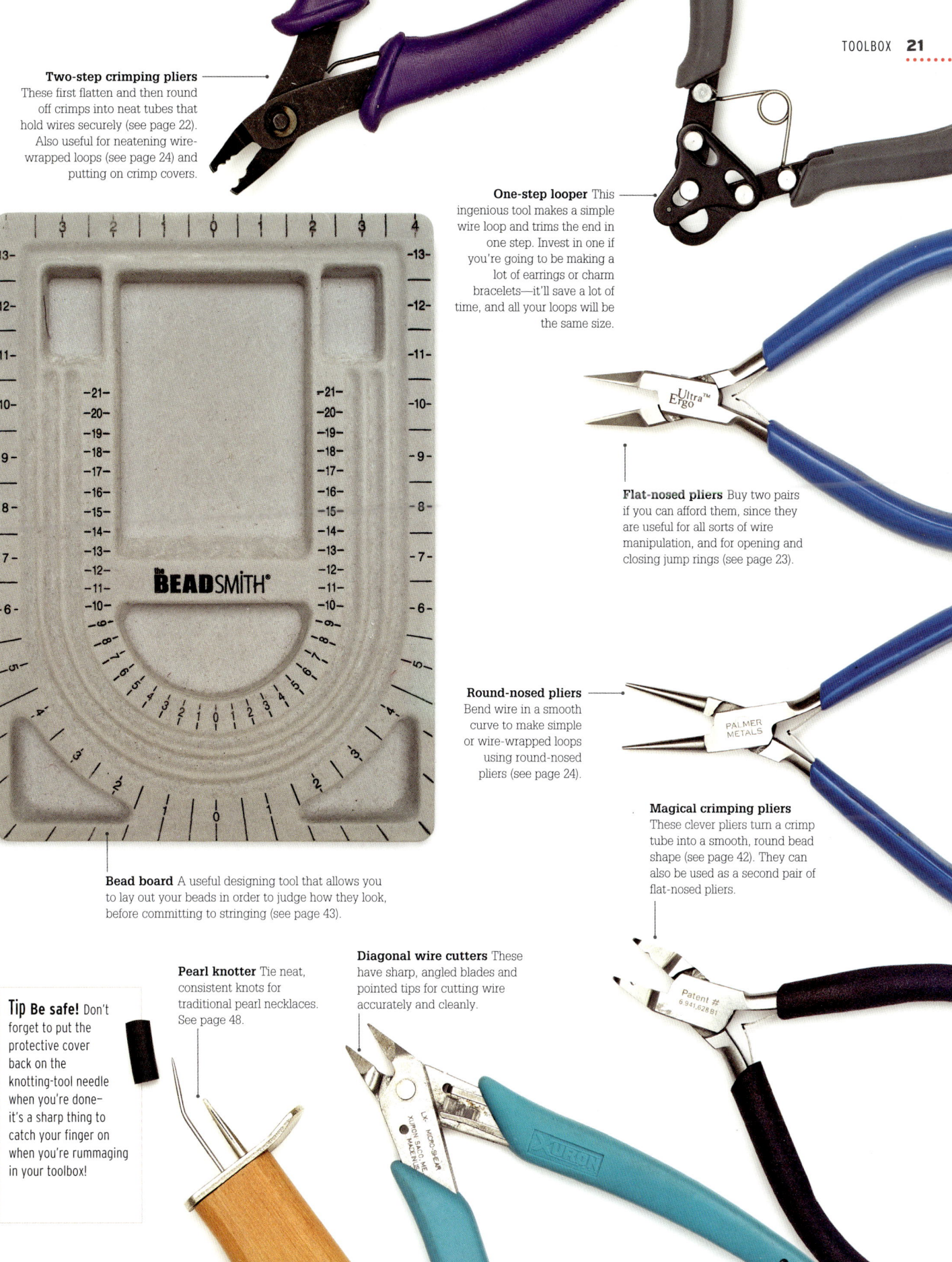

**Two-step crimping pliers** These first flatten and then round off crimps into neat tubes that hold wires securely (see page 22). Also useful for neatening wire-wrapped loops (see page 24) and putting on crimp covers.

**One-step looper** This ingenious tool makes a simple wire loop and trims the end in one step. Invest in one if you're going to be making a lot of earrings or charm bracelets—it'll save a lot of time, and all your loops will be the same size.

**Flat-nosed pliers** Buy two pairs if you can afford them, since they are useful for all sorts of wire manipulation, and for opening and closing jump rings (see page 23).

**Round-nosed pliers** Bend wire in a smooth curve to make simple or wire-wrapped loops using round-nosed pliers (see page 24).

**Magical crimping pliers** These clever pliers turn a crimp tube into a smooth, round bead shape (see page 42). They can also be used as a second pair of flat-nosed pliers.

**Bead board** A useful designing tool that allows you to lay out your beads in order to judge how they look, before committing to stringing (see page 43).

**Pearl knotter** Tie neat, consistent knots for traditional pearl necklaces. See page 48.

**Diagonal wire cutters** These have sharp, angled blades and pointed tips for cutting wire accurately and cleanly.

**Tip Be safe!** Don't forget to put the protective cover back on the knotting-tool needle when you're done—it's a sharp thing to catch your finger on when you're rummaging in your toolbox!

# Techniques

As you work through the projects in the book, you'll learn plenty of techniques. Here are some of the most basic and useful.

Alongside each technique you'll find references to one or two projects that use it, so you can go straight to those projects and refine your skills.

## TECHNIQUE: ONE-STEP LOOPER TOOL

Project: Summer nights earrings, page 46

 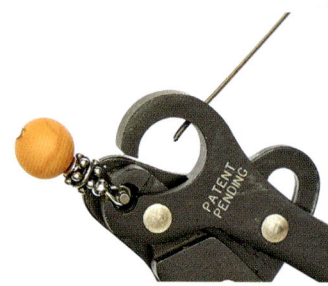

**STEP 1**
String two or three beads on a headpin. Insert the end of the wire into your one-step looper so the beads are close to the bottom jaw of the tool.

**STEP 2**
Squeeze the handles of the one-step looper. The tool will form a simple loop in the headpin and trim the end of the wire. (If you don't have this tool, follow the Simple loops technique; see page 23.)

## TECHNIQUE: OVERHAND KNOT

Projects: Talisman pendant, page 32; Wave pendant, page 36

   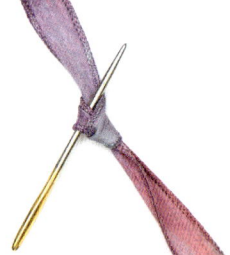

**STEP 1**
Form a loop in a length of ribbon, cord, or thread by crossing one end over the other.

**STEP 2**
Take the free end to the back and bring it up through the loop.

**STEP 3**
Pull gently to tighten the knot.

**STEP 4**
You can use an awl or a large needle to move the knot to the right place in the ribbon. Insert the awl into the loop before tightening the knot, and slide the knot along the ribbon.

## TECHNIQUE: CRIMPING

Project: Rugged rocks necklace, page 88

 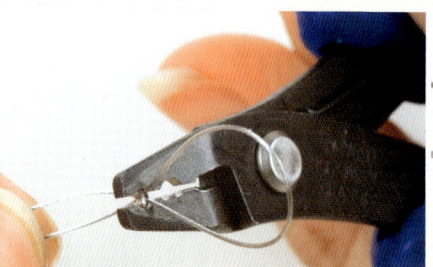 

**STEP 1**
Press your crimp using the notch nearest the handle of your pliers—this crimps the center of the bead and turns your crimp into a figure-eight shape. The aim is to get one piece of flexible wire into each section of the crimp.

**STEP 2**
Move your crimp to the notch nearest the point of your pliers. You now need to turn it so that it sits with one wire above the other. Press down with your pliers to round the crimp. You can then rotate your crimp in the pliers and re-crimp to fully round it.

**STEP 3**
When crimping pliers are used, the end result is a much rounder and neater crimp with no sharp edges. You can also use magical crimping pliers; see page 42.

## TECHNIQUE: BEAD SPINNER

Projects: Beach love beads, page 38; Light my fire necklace, page 106

### STEP 1
Fill the bowl with at least 20g of your chosen seed bead color or mixture. Thread the curved needle (which comes with the spinner) with a yard or so of nylon beading thread. Tie a single bead to the free end of the thread, using a single overhand knot (see page 22). This stop bead will be removed at the end.

### STEP 2
Hold the tip of the needle in the loose beads and spin the spinner toward the needle with your nondominant hand.

### STEP 3
The beads will jump onto the needle. You might need to adjust the angle at which you're holding the needle, in order to make this process more efficient.

### STEP 4
When the needle's full, stop spinning and push the beads down the thread. Repeat until your strand is the desired length. If you're not using the strand straight away, tie another single stop bead onto the end with the needle before removing the thread from the needle.

## TECHNIQUE: OPENING AND CLOSING JUMP RINGS

Projects: Wildflower wrap bracelet, page 50; Sunny morning bracelet, page 56

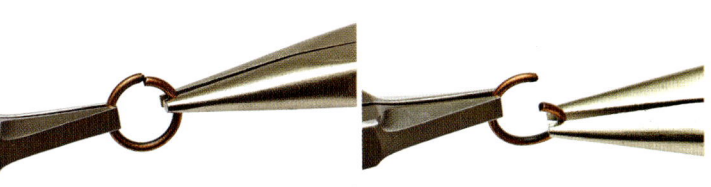   

### STEP 1
Grip the jump ring with two pairs of pliers, with the ring opening at the top.

### STEP 2
Twist the ring, don't pull it: move one end toward you and the other end away, until the opening is wide enough.

### STEP 3
Attach the desired finding or component to the opened ring.

### STEP 4
Again with two pairs of pliers, twist the ring ends back toward each other to close the gap. Move the ends back and forth until the gap is completely closed.

## TECHNIQUE: SIMPLE LOOPS

Projects: Simple pleasures earrings, page 28; Crystal cascade necklace, page 64

### STEP 1
With flat-nosed pliers, grasp the wire just above your final bead and bend at 90 degrees.

### STEP 2
Use diagonal wire cutters to trim the wire to ⁵⁄₈" (15mm).

### STEP 3
Grasp the free end in round-nosed pliers and rotate the pliers to turn a smooth loop in the wire. Be careful to keep that 90-degree bend.

### STEP 4
Use flat-nosed pliers to adjust the loop if necessary.

## TECHNIQUE: MAKING A TRIANGLE BAIL FOR A TOP-DRILLED BEAD

Project: Simple pleasures earrings, page 28

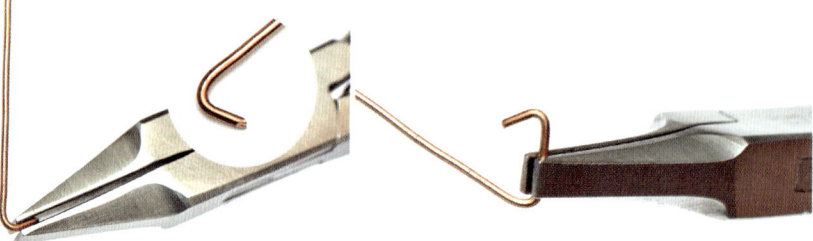
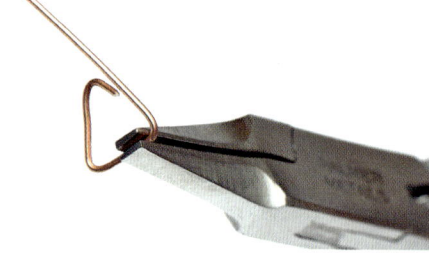

**STEP 1**
Take a straight piece of medium-gauge wire. Grasp the end 1/16" (2mm) of the wire with flat-nosed pliers and make a 60-degree bend.

**STEP 2**
Grasp the wire 1/4" (6mm) from the first bend and make another 60-degree bend on the same plane.

**STEP 3**
Make a third 60-degree bend 1/4" (6mm) from the second bend. You should now have a triangle shape.

## TECHNIQUE: WIRE-WRAPPED LOOPS

Projects: Wave pendant, page 36; Rustic romance bracelet, page 60

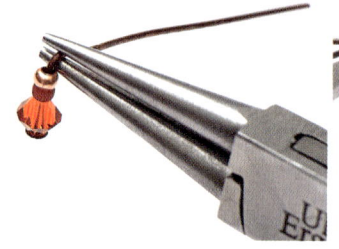
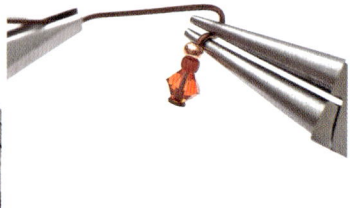

**STEP 1**
String your chosen beads onto a headpin. Hold the pin with the tip of the round-nosed pliers approximately 1/32" (1mm) above the beads. Bend the free end of the wire away from you until the bend is approximately 90 degrees.

**STEP 2**
Holding the end of the wire in the flat-nosed pliers, bend the wire toward you around the top jaw of the round-nosed pliers without losing the 90-degree bend made in the previous step.

**STEP 3**
Move this semicircular bend onto the bottom jaw of the pliers. Bend the free end of wire around, under the bottom jaw of the pliers, and back toward you, to complete the loop.

**STEP 4**
Still holding the loop, move the round-nosed pliers into your other hand. Use flat-nosed pliers to coil the free end of wire around the short vertical length between the 90-degree bend and the top of the beads.

## TECHNIQUE: WIRE-WRAPPING RIBBON

Project: Silk and stone bracelet, page 86

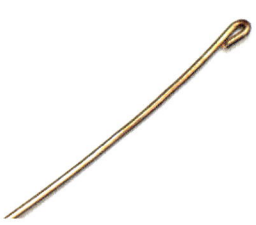
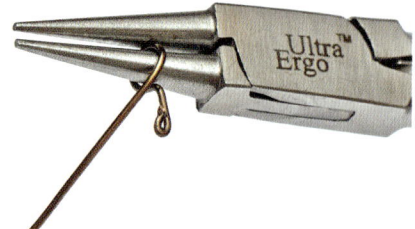

**STEP 1**
Cut a piece of wire approximately 3" (7.5cm) long. Fold over the end and squash with flat-nosed pliers.

**STEP 2**
Leaving a short vertical end of no more than 1/4" (6mm), bend the wire at 90 degrees and wrap around your round-nosed pliers, just as though you were starting a regular wrapped loop. Make the loop a little larger than you would for an earring dangle. Don't start wrapping yet.

**STEP 3**
Fold over the very end of a piece of ribbon and trap it between the loop and the short vertical end of the wire. Squash with flat-nosed pliers to hold the ribbon in place.

**STEP 4**
Trim the wire ¹⁄₁₆" (1.5mm) from the final bend.

**STEP 5**
Use two pairs of flat-nosed pliers to pull the ends apart. Push one end into each side of the hole in the bead.

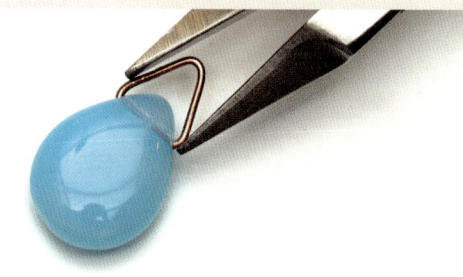

**STEP 6**
Use flat-nosed pliers to push the ends together again until the bead is held securely.

**STEP 5**
Wrap the wire around again. Twice should do it unless your gap is very large. Try to keep the wraps as neat as possible.

**STEP 6**
Use diagonal wire cutters to trim the end of the wire as close to the coil as possible.

**STEP 7**
Use the round notch in a pair of two-step crimping pliers to tidy up the loose end by pressing it gently into the coil. Be very careful not to break the beads.

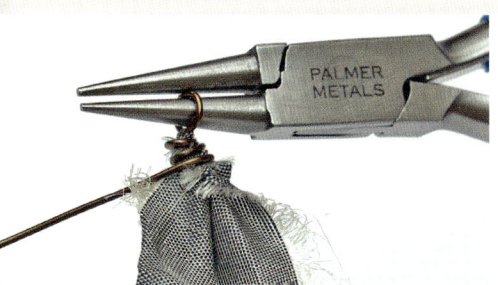

**STEP 4**
Replace the loop on your round-nosed pliers and wrap the long end of the wire around both the ribbon and the short vertical end. It's best to use your fingers for this. Don't wrap the wire too tightly.

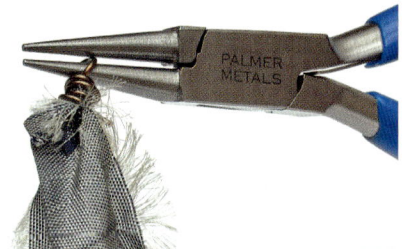

**STEP 5**
Wrap the wire over itself, up and down, to make a rustic-looking knot, instead of a neat, wrapped coil.

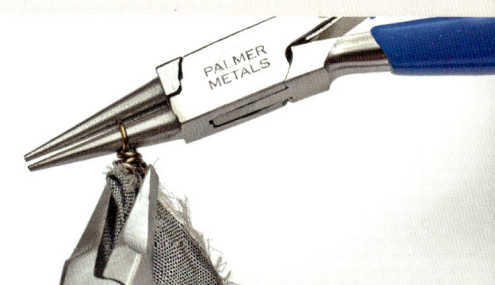

**STEP 6**
Use flat-nosed pliers to wrap the last ¹⁄₂" (1.2cm) of wire. Press the cut end into the knot and make sure it's well tucked in so there are no sharp ends to catch.

# Chapter 2
# Projects

Whether you choose just a few, or decide to try them all, each of these designs will enhance your beading skills. There's something for everyone here, from a simple pendant to a multistranded collar, from chunky stone nuggets to elegant crystals, from statement focals to tiny seed beads. Pick your favorite and start creating!

## YOU WILL NEED

### BEAD BOX

Choose a selection to make
a single pair of earrings
(see captions):

- Pairs of 15mm beads, such as
  lampwork glass, freshwater pearl,
  seaglass, dichroic glass, crystal
- Selection of 4-6mm beads
- 11º metal seed beads
- 8º and 11º glass seed beads
- Pairs of charms
- Pairs of 6mm metal flower spacers

### HARDWARE

**Essential**

- Pairs of 2" (50mm) headpins
- Pairs of earring wires

**For varying your designs**

- Pair of 12mm ornate silver bead caps
- Pairs of 2" (50mm) eyepins
- 4mm and 6mm jump rings
- Triangle bails, or medium-gauge
  copper or brass wire

### TOOLKIT

- Flat-nosed pliers (2 pairs)
- Diagonal wire cutters
- Round-nosed pliers
- One-step looper (optional)

# Simple pleasures earrings

Earrings are beady instant
gratification. Learn how to
choose and combine beads with
findings and the very simplest
wirework techniques to create
these little treasures.

Make the small beads
a more intense shade.
This will give the
illusion of more color to
the seaglass, too.

## SEAGLASS

**See it GROW**

Make sure there is at
least ⅝" (15mm) of wire
above your beads so
there's enough to make
a nicely shaped loop.

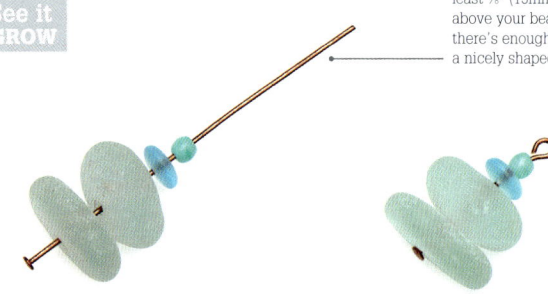

**STAGE 1** String your chosen
beads onto headpins (for design
inspiration, see the captions for
each pair of earrings).

**STAGE 2** Make a simple loop at
the top of each headpin using
pliers or a one-step looper (see
page 22).

**STAGE 3** Hold the hook part of
an earring wire in one hand and
use flat-nosed pliers to open the
loop at the bottom. Twist, don't
pull, otherwise your loop will go
out of shape.

**STAGE 4** Hook the opened
earring wire into the loop at the
top of the headpin. Use the pliers
to twist the earring wire closed
again. Repeat to make the
second earring.

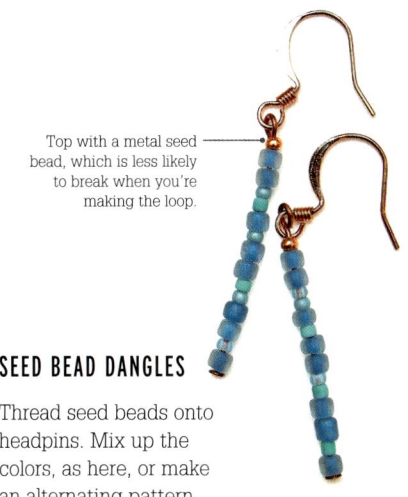

Top with a metal seed bead, which is less likely to break when you're making the loop.

## SEED BEAD DANGLES

Thread seed beads onto headpins. Mix up the colors, as here, or make an alternating pattern.

## PEARDROPS

Use bought triangle bails, or make your own (see page 24) to make earrings using top-drilled beads. Attach to the earring wire using two jump rings.

Notice how each jump ring is at 90 degrees to the previous one. If you used just one jump ring for these starfish charms, they would hang sideways. A second ring brings them back into the correct alignment.

## CHARMS

Use two jump rings to attach each charm, one ring attached to the top of the charm and the second ring to attach the first ring to an earring wire.

You can twist the loop at the bottom of the eyepin to ensure that your charms hang facing the front. Hold the top loop in one pair of pliers and the bottom loop in another pair, and twist gently until the loops are aligned.

## EYEPINS

Using eyepins instead of headpins, follow the steps for the basic earring, then use jump rings to attach charms to the loops at the bottoms of the eyepins.

## FLORAL

String a 4mm pearl and a few seed beads, then a cup-shaped lampwork flower, a 4mm glass round, and a metal seed bead.

The pearl should peep out below the petals.

Use thinner-gauge headpins because most pearls and coral tips have tiny holes.

## PEARLS

Add a few coral tips to a pearl earring for a splash of complementary color.

## LAMPWORK DUO

Pick two pairs of handmade glass beads, say 6mm and 10mm. Choose some seed beads that match or complement the lampwork beads— here, gunmetal 8º seeds mirror the bumps on the beads. String a seed bead, a small lampwork bead, a 4mm crystal bicone, a big lampwork bead, a seed bead, and a metal seed bead.

Crystal bicones are handy for use with lampwork beads because they fit nicely into the dimples that you'll find at the ends of any well-made "lampie." This effectively makes the holes smaller and stops the beads from wobbling around on the pin.

Use black seed beads to further contrast with the bright colors of the dichroic glass.

## DICHROIC

Make the most of these intensely vivid beads by framing them with silver. A 6mm flower spacer is strung below each dichroic bead, with an elaborate Bali-style bead cap on top.

**Tip Get to know a variety of beads** Notice how some beads are heavier than others; this is particularly important for earrings because you really don't want them to be uncomfortably heavy. Where possible, choose lightweight alternatives: for example, acrylic faux pearls are lighter than glass crystal ones, and a hollow or "blown" glass bead will weigh much less than a solid one. Polymer clay is another nice material for earring beads.

**BEAD BOX**
- 7 Bali silver 8mm ball spacers (A)
- 12 silver 2mm rounds (B)
- 6 pale blue 12 x 16mm amazonite rectangular pillows (C)
- 2 Bali silver 4 x 5mm flower spacers (D)

**HARDWARE**
- .018" (.46mm) flexible beading wire
- 2 silver 2 x 2mm crimp tubes
- 2 silver 4mm wire guardians
- 2 silver 4mm plain round crimp covers
- 2 silver 4mm jump rings
- 22mm silver filigree square toggle, or clasp of your choice

**TOOLKIT**
- Diagonal wire cutters
- Bead stoppers or paper clips
- Flat-nosed pliers (2 pairs)
- Crimping pliers

**Finished bracelet:** Approximately 8" (20cm) long

# Pacific bracelet

Inspired by the soft sea-green color of amazonite beads, this timeless bracelet is a very simple design. As you create it, you will learn the tips and techniques that turn a basic piece of stringing into something special and beautiful. Practice these skills and you'll soon be stringing like a professional!

**See it GROW**

**STAGE 1** Cut a 10" (25cm) length of beading wire. Put a bead stopper or paper clip near one end. String beads in the following order: [A, B, C, B]. Do this six times.

**STAGE 2** String a final A bead. Check the length around your wrist, allowing just over 1" (2.5cm) for the clasp. Add or subtract beads if necessary.

**STAGE 3** String a crimp tube, a D bead, and a wire guardian. Go back through the last few beads. Pull the end of the wire until no slack is visible in the loop of the wire guardian.

## FLEXIBILITY

Why didn't you just string the pillow beads together? Why does the design need those fiddly little silver beads in between? Well, take a look:

The pillow beads look lovely all together, but when you curve them around to make a bracelet, there is a problem. If the tension is loose enough to make the curve, the bare wire shows in between the beads; if the tension is tight so the beads are close together, the strand won't bend enough to go around the wrist.

Adding big ball spacers goes some way to solving the problem, but the holes in those big balls are quite large and they wobble around on the wire. Some wire inevitably still shows when you bend the beads into a circle.

The tiny silver beads fix the problem. They stabilize the bigger holes of the ball spacers, and they give the strand the flexibility it needs to curve into a bracelet. This is why you'll notice a lot of small beads in between the bigger ones in projects throughout this book, particularly bracelets (the curve on a necklace isn't so tight, so it doesn't need to be quite as flexible).

STAGE 4

STAGE 5

STAGE 6

**STAGE 4** Secure the crimp with crimping pliers (see page 22), and trim the end of the cable.

Leave a little gap when crimping

**STAGE 5** Remove the bead stopper. Finish the other end as for Stage 4, allowing $\frac{1}{32}$–$\frac{1}{16}$" (1–2mm) of slack in the wire between the crimp and the strand of beads. This will give room for the crimp covers without making the whole bracelet too rigid.

**STAGE 6** Use the larger notch of the two-step crimping pliers to close a crimp cover carefully around each crimp.

A cover neatly disguises your crimp.

**Tip A matching pair** Matching earrings are easily made using the techniques you learned in the Simple pleasures earrings (see page 28). String C, D, B onto a headpin and form a simple loop at the top. Do this twice, attach earwires, and you're done. And, of course, if you have more amazonite beads you can string a longer length for a necklace–perhaps with the big ball spacers just at the front, and the smaller flower spacers at the back, so the necklace isn't too heavy.

STAGE 7

**STAGE 7** Use two pairs of flat-nosed pliers to open a 4mm jump ring (see page 23) and attach one half of the clasp to one end of the bracelet.

**STAGE 8** Attach the other half of the clasp to the other end with the remaining jump ring.

STAGE 8

# Talisman pendant

A definite case of "less is more," this pendant necklace has a very simple, primitive style. The striking two-tone handmade Greek ceramic beads need little more than a length of lace to show them off. Learn to tie two basic and very useful knots, and how to attach a metal clasp, and you'll be looking like a Grecian goddess in no time.

## YOU WILL NEED

### BEAD BOX
- 1 copper frost 40mm ceramic pendant
- 4 copper frost 12mm ceramic round beads
- 2 copper frost 16 x 4mm ceramic cornflake beads

### HARDWARE
- 41" (104cm) brown 2mm faux suede lace
- 2 copper 4 x 2mm ribbon end crimps
- 2 copper 6mm jump rings
- 1 copper 12mm hook clasp

### TOOLKIT
- Sharp scissors
- Flat-nosed pliers (2 pairs)

**Finished necklace:**
Approximately 22" (55cm) long, excluding pendant

STAGE 1

STAGE 2

STAGE 3

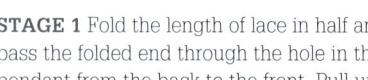

**STAGE 1** Fold the length of lace in half and pass the folded end through the hole in the pendant from the back to the front. Pull until you have a loop.

**STAGE 2** Put both ends of the lace through the loop and pull until the loop is snug against the pendant. Congratulations! You have just tied a lark's-head knot.

**STAGE 3** Measure approximately 1" (2.5cm) along the lace and make a loop. Pass the end of the lace through the loop and tighten the overhand knot you've just tied, holding the lace at the 1" (2.5cm) point so the knot stays in place.

**STAGE 4** String a round bead and push it down to the knot. Tie another overhand knot just above it to keep it in place. Repeat Stages 3 and 4 on the other side of the necklace.

**STAGE 5** Measure 1" (2.5cm) along the cord from one of the round beads and tie another overhand knot. String a cornflake bead and tie a second knot above it, leaving a ½" (1.2cm) gap between the knots to allow the bead to rotate into a comfortable position when the necklace is worn. Repeat on the other side of the necklace.

**STAGE 6** Add a second round bead on each side, by repeating Stages 3 and 4 at a distance of 1" (2.5cm) from the cornflake bead.

STAGE 4

STAGE 5

STAGE 6

**Tip Adapt the design** This project will work with any large-holed pendants or beads. The hole in the pendant should be at least 4mm wide to allow for a double thickness of the lace. The holes in the other beads should be 2-4mm so the lace will pass through easily but a single knot will be big enough to hold the bead in place. If you want more beads in the necklace, remember to add an extra 1½" (4cm) of lace for every knot, or 3" (7.5cm) for each additional bead.

**STAGE 7** Hold the necklace up and adjust the positions of the beads and knots if necessary. Trim both ends to the same length. Use flat-nosed pliers to attach a ribbon end crimp (see Technique, below) to each end.

**STAGE 8** Use two pairs of pliers to open a jump ring (see page 23). Attach to one of the ribbon end crimps and close the ring. Open the second jump ring and use it to attach the hook clasp to the other end of the necklace.

These crimps are also handy for finishing the ends of short sections of ribbon or lace to be used as components in a necklace, or if you want to attach tassels or dangles to the ends of ribbons without having to tie knots.

STAGE 7

STAGE 8

## TECHNIQUE: RIBBON END CRIMPS

**STEP 1**
Trim the ends of the lace square across with sharp scissors.

**STEP 2**
Push one end of the lace into the channel of a ribbon end crimp.

**STEP 3**
Use flat-nosed pliers to carefully push one wing of the crimp down onto the lace, and squash it as flat as you can.

**STEP 4**
Push the other wing down on top of the first and, again, squash it flat. Pull gently but firmly on the lace to make sure that it's held securely by the crimp. If it slips, squash the crimp some more.

# Teardrop trio necklaces

This trio of necklaces can be layered or worn singly. A chunky heart pendant, a formal teardrop necklet, and a random string of glass and pearls all tone together to make a fashionable statement for any occasion.

**Tip Balanced additions** Size isn't important here; it's the balance that counts when you're layering. Pick necklace lengths that are comfortable for you. If you want to be able to adjust them, add an extender chain to the ring end of each clasp. There's no need to stop at three: add more chains, chunky beach glass, a string of pearls... just make sure that the colors relate to the other necklaces in the set.

## YOU WILL NEED

### BEAD BOX

- 6 silver 4 x 5mm flower spacers (A)
- 1 aqua 30 x 25mm handmade lampwork glass heart focal
- 140 (approx.) Capri blue matte transparent 8º Japanese seed beads (B)
- 85 (approx.) silver 11º metal seed beads (C)
- 11 milky aquamarine 16 x 12mm flat top-drilled glass peardrops (D)
- 20 aquamarine frost 9 x 6mm top-drilled glass teardrops (E)
- 16 aquamarine AB 6 x 4mm top-drilled glass teardrops (F)
- 14 white 6 x 2mm flat round keshi pearls
- 20 (approx.) aquamarine transparent 6º Japanese seed beads
- 8 white 6-7mm round freshwater pearls
- 20 (approx.) dark aquamarine matte 6mm glass rondelles

### HARDWARE

- 1 silver 1" (25mm) headpin
- 1 silver 8mm jump ring
- 1 silver ready-made 18" (45cm) fine curb chain with clasp
- .018" (.46mm) flexible beading wire
- 4 silver 2 x 2mm crimp tubes
- 2 silver 3mm jump rings
- 2 silver 4mm jump rings
- 2 silver 10mm lobster claw clasps

### TOOLKIT

- Round-nosed pliers
- Flat-nosed pliers (2 pairs)
- Diagonal wire cutters
- Bead stopper or paper clip
- Magical crimping pliers

**See it GROW**

**PENDANT**

**STAGE 1** String A, the heart, B, and C on the headpin. Make a wire-wrapped loop (see page 24). Attach the 8mm jump ring to the loop (see page 23) and string it onto the ready-made chain.

**Finished size:** Pendant chain 18" (45cm); teardrop necklace 16" (40cm); random necklace 18" (45cm)

## TEARDROP NECKLACE

**STAGE 2** This is strung from the center outward. Cut a piece of beading wire approximately 19" (48cm) long. String a peardrop and slide it to the center. Now string [C, B, E, B, C, D] a total of five times on each side.

**STAGE 3** String [C, B, E, B, C, F] a total of three times on each side.

**STAGE 4** String [C, three Bs, C, F] a total of three times on each side. Finish each end with a metal seed bead, 3 Capri blue seed beads, a crimp tube, and a final Capri blue bead.

**STAGE 5** Put a bead stopper or paper clip on one end of the wire. Pass the free end of the wire back through the last 5 beads (including the crimp) and pull until only a small loop remains. Secure the crimp with crimping pliers (see page 22), trim the surplus wire, and use a 3mm jump ring to attach a lobster claw clasp (see page 23). Crimp the other end in the same way and attach a 4mm jump ring.

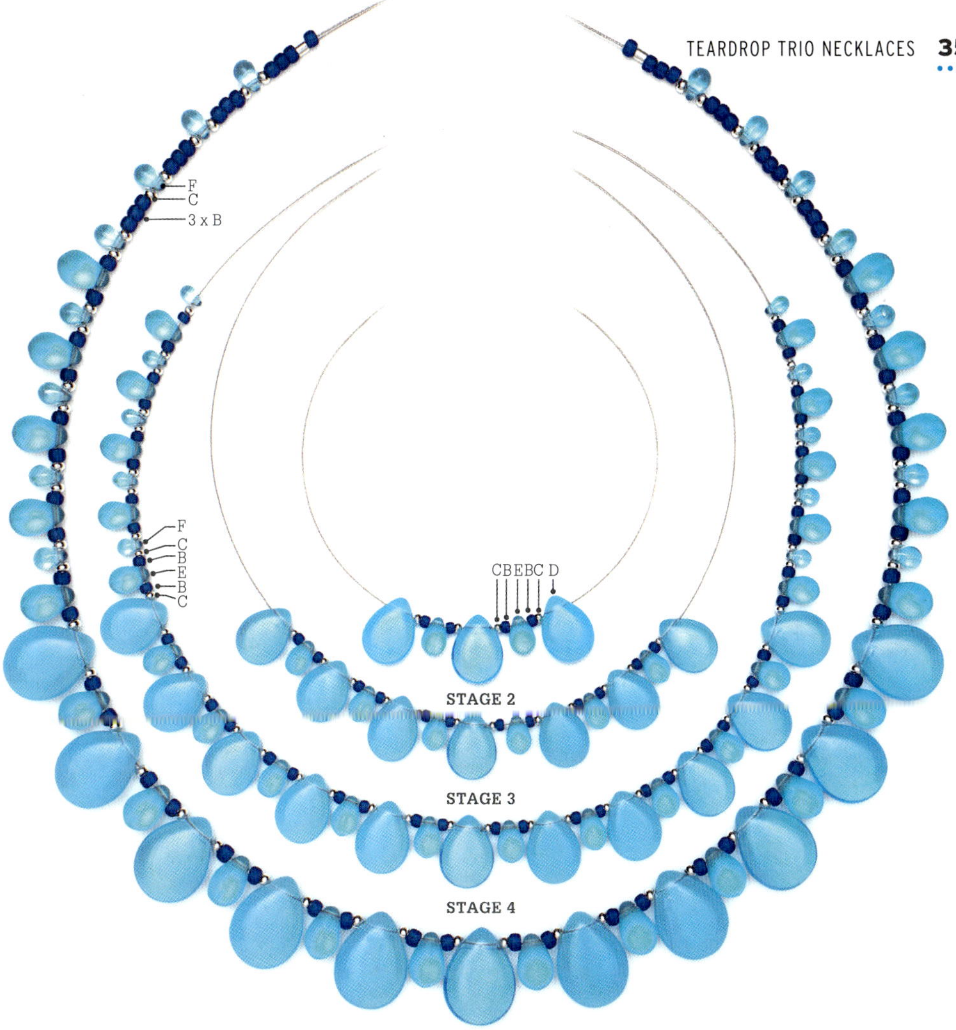

F
C
3 x B

F
C
B
E
B
C

CBEBC D

**STAGE 2**

**STAGE 3**

**STAGE 4**

### RANDOMNESS

Randomness is something you will encounter in many of the projects in this book. It's not hard to do and it adds a lovely dimension of unpredictability. A bead board is a handy way to mix your beads so that the distribution of the stand-out beads (in this case the pearls) is approximately even along the length. To make the necklace pleasing to the eye, you need to unify the design as well as the colors. If you look closely at the random strand you'll see that certain design elements are repeated such as **G** the silver seed bead either side of the small teardrops, **H** the keshi pearls in pairs, and **I** the aqua seed beads either side of the round pearls. These help to tie the whole design together in a satisfying way.

I    I         G  G    H      G        G

## RANDOM STRING

**STAGE 6** This is strung starting at one end. Cut a piece of beading wire approximately 21" (53cm) long. Put a bead stopper or paper clip on one end. Lay out your remaining beads on a bead board or tray and arrange until you are happy with the distribution (see Randomness, left).

**STAGE 7** String beads in small groups, aiming for a random but balanced effect, until your strand is approximately 17" (43cm) long.

**STAGE 8** Finish each end with C, three Bs, a crimp tube, and a final B bead. Secure the crimps and attach the clasp as in Stage 5.

**STAGE 7**

**STAGE 8**

## YOU WILL NEED

### BEAD BOX
- 1 blue and green 25-35mm lentil-shaped art glass focal bead
- 2 silver 4 x 5mm flower spacers
- 1 silver 11º metal seed bead
- 4 silver 5mm twisted ring spacers
- 1 silver 9 x 6mm wave-patterned bead with 3mm hole

### HARDWARE
- 1 silver 3" (75mm) headpin
- 1 silver 18mm pendant bail
- 1 blue-green 3'3" (1m) length of handpainted silk crêpe-de-chine ribbon

### TOOLKIT
- Round-nosed pliers
- Flat-nosed pliers
- Diagonal wire cutters

**Finished necklace:** Adjustable between 18" (45cm) and 24" (60cm) long

# Wave pendant

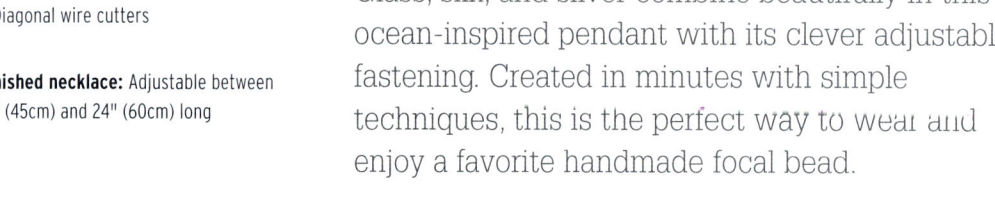

Glass, silk, and silver combine beautifully in this ocean-inspired pendant with its clever adjustable fastening. Created in minutes with simple techniques, this is the perfect way to wear and enjoy a favorite handmade focal bead.

See it GROW

**STAGE 1** String a flower spacer, the focal bead, another flower spacer, and the seed bead onto the headpin.

**STAGE 2** Make the first stage of a wire-wrapped loop (see page 24), stopping as soon as you've made a loop. Slide the loop of the pendant bail onto the wire loop and continue with the wrapping part of the technique.

**STAGE 3** Trim the end of the wire. You now have a pendant attached to the bail. (You can just make a simple loop if you prefer [see page 23], but a wrapped loop is more secure.)

**STAGE 4** String the bail onto the ribbon and slide it to the center.

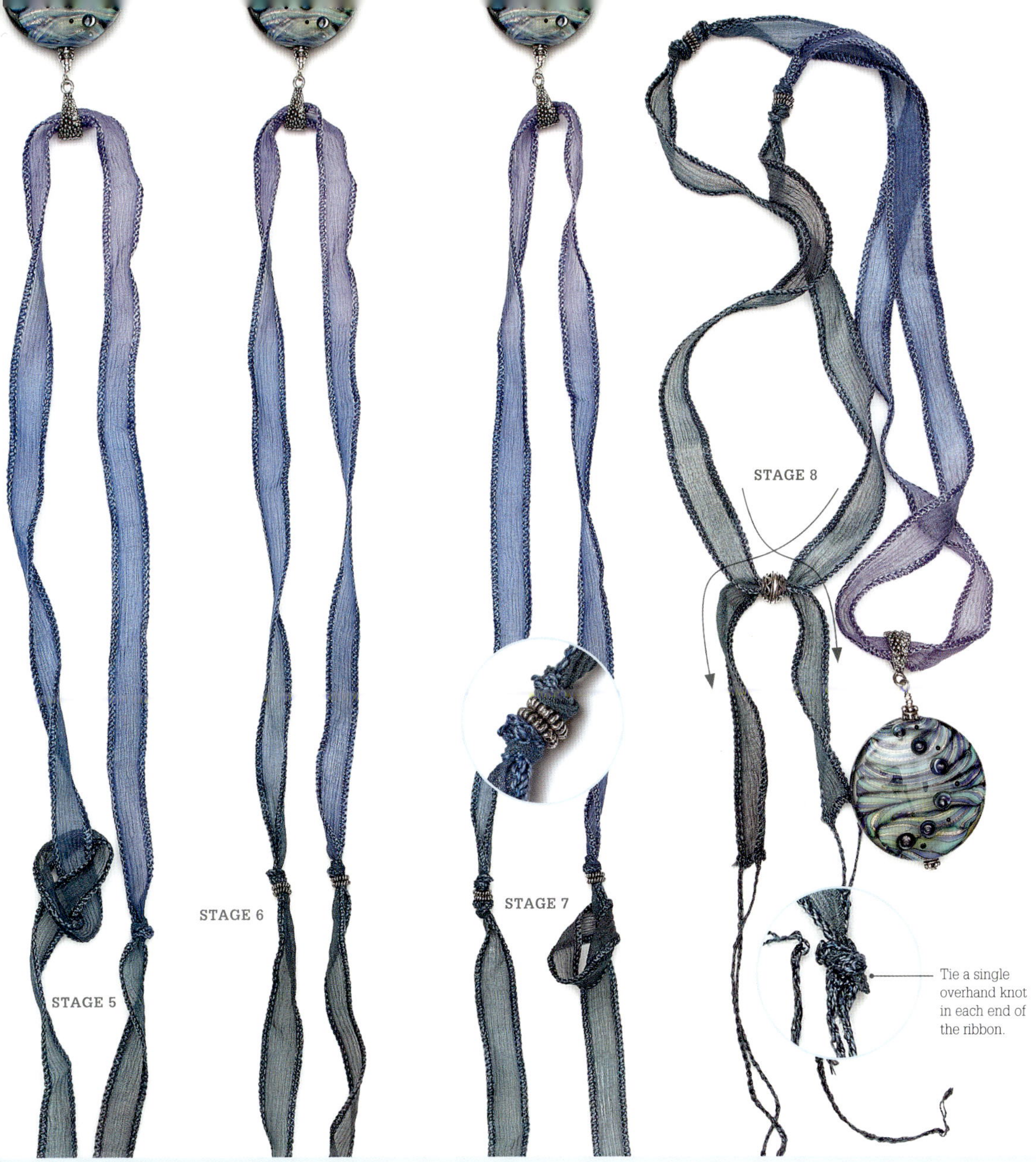

**STAGE 5** Tie an overhand knot (see page 22) in each side of the ribbon approximately 7–8" (18–20cm) from the pendant.

**STAGE 6** String two ring spacers onto each end of the ribbon.

**STAGE 7** Tie another overhand knot after the spacers. These knots and beads will prevent the necklace from pulling too tight.

**STAGE 8** String the wave-patterned bead onto one end of the ribbon. Pass the other end of the ribbon through the bead in the opposite direction. Tie a single overhand knot in each end of the ribbon so it can't be accidentally pulled out of the bead.

**Tip** Finishing ribbon ends

The ends of handmade silk ribbons are usually already finished, but if the ends of your ribbon are raw, you can use knots to finish them, or fold the ends and stitch neatly, or just cut at a 45-degree angle and accept some degree of fraying.

STAGE 8

STAGE 5

STAGE 6

STAGE 7

Tie a single overhand knot in each end of the ribbon.

## TECHNIQUE: MAKING A PENDANT WITHOUT A PENDANT BAIL

**STEP 1**
String a crystal either side of your focal bead, for sparkle and stability. Finish with a metal seed bead to avoid the crystal cracking when you make your wrapped loop.

**STEP 2**
Make a wrapped loop, making the loop part rather larger than you would if making earrings or small dangles, to allow the pendant to hang freely.

**STEP 3**
See how the crystals sit in the dimples of the lampwork bead and keep it from rattling around on the headpin.

**STEP 4**
Instead of the bail, use jump rings to hang your pendant from its ribbon. Simply open a 4mm jump ring (see page 23) and pass it through both a 6mm soldered jump ring and your wrapped loop. Close the 4mm jump ring.

**STEP 5**
For added security, add a second 4mm jump ring beside the first. Now put the ribbon through the 6mm jump ring.

**LENTIL BEADCAPS**
You can also purchase special lentil beadcaps, which are shaped to fit lentil focals. This creates a neat finish without the need for extra beads.

# Beach love beads

Making a long necklace with tiny seed beads is surprisingly quick and easy when you use a bead spinner. Create several strands and add a focal pendant for a casual summertime look.

**See it GROW**

**STAGE 1** Cut a yard or so (approximately 1m) of nylon beading thread and thread onto the curved needle that comes with the bead spinner. String one seed bead and slide to within 3" (7.5cm) of the end. This will be your stop bead. Tie it on with a single overhand knot (see page 22). It will be removed later.

**STAGE 2** Fill the bowl of the bead spinner with seed beads and start spinning (see page 23). Every so often, stop spinning and add an accent bead or a little cluster of heishi (you may need to remove the curved needle and thread a beading needle instead to do this).

STAGE 1

Do remember to tie a stop bead to the end of your thread before starting to spin. Otherwise you'll pick up the completed strand only to watch the beads slide off and scatter far and wide!

STAGE 2

## YOU WILL NEED

### BEAD BOX
- At least 20g of mixed 11° seed beads in "beachy" colors–add a few 8° beads to give a more organic texture
- A few small (4-6mm) accent beads such as pearls or shells
- 20-30 natural shell 4mm heishi disks
- Undrilled shell donut, 2" (50mm) in diameter

### TOOLKIT
- Nylon beading thread
- Scissors
- Bead spinner
- Beading needle

**Finished necklace:** 24" (60cm) long

Tie both ends of thread together with a double or triple overhand knot.

STAGE 3

STAGE 4

Make sure the "bead soup" in the spinner is filled to cover at least one third of the spinner bottom, as bead spinning with a very small amount is a thankless task.

**STAGE 3** When the strung beads are long enough to fit easily over your head, stop spinning and take the curved needle off the thread. Remove the stop bead from the other end and tie both ends of thread together with a double or triple overhand knot.

**STAGE 4** Thread a beading needle with one end of the beaded thread and stitch through a couple of inches of the strung beads. Trim the end. Repeat with the other end.

STAGE 5

---

**Tips Experiments with color**
Make each strand a subtly different color by adding more seed beads to the mix in the spinner after completing a strand. Even a few flecks of a contrast color can change the whole appearance of a necklace.

**Suitable storage** Store your "love beads" on a hook or clothes hanger so they don't get tangled.

---

**STAGE 5** Make another necklace the same length as the first, then make a third one that is 1" (2.5cm) longer.

**STAGE 6** Use a lark's-head knot (see Technique) to attach the longest necklace to the shell donut. Wear the necklaces singly or as a group. And why stop at three? You could make many more.

STAGE 6

---

## TECHNIQUE: LARK'S HEAD KNOT

**STEP 1**
We've shown cord for clarity, but this technique works just as well with a necklace of seed beads. Fold the necklace to make a narrow loop. If you're using cord or ribbon, fold it in half.

**STEP 2**
String your pendant or donut onto the folded end.

**STEP 3**
Pull the other end of the necklace, or the free ends of the cord, through the loop formed by the folded end.

**STEP 4**
Gently pull on the beads or cord to tighten the knot.

**STEP 5**
Note that the appearance will be different depending on whether you push the folded end through from front to back, or from back to front. You can use this as a design feature.

## YOU WILL NEED

### BEAD BOX
- 37 caramel 9mm glass scallop beads (A)
- 70 (approx.) blue Picasso 8º seed beads (B)
- 70 (approx.) silver 2mm round beads (C)
- 13 beige Picasso 9 x 6mm glass faceted rondelles (D)
- 10 milky tortoiseshell 16mm glass ammonite beads (E)
- 25 coral pink Picasso 9mm fluted firepolished glass bicones (F)

### HARDWARE
- 15 silver 2" (50mm) headpins
- .018" (.46mm) flexible beading wire
- 8 silver 2 x 2mm crimp tubes
- 3 silver 7mm soldered (closed) jump rings
- 2 silver 4mm wire guardians
- 4 silver 6mm jump rings
- 1 silver 15mm lobster claw clasp or necklace hook
- 2 silver 2" (50mm) eyepins
- 1 pair silver earwires

### TOOLKIT
- Round-nosed pliers
- Flat-nosed pliers (2 pairs)
- Diagonal wire cutters
- Bead stoppers or paper clips
- Magical crimping pliers (or crimping pliers)
- Bead board (optional but useful)

**Finished necklace:** Approximately 19" (48cm) long

**Finished earrings:** Approximately 2" (5cm)

# Jurassic Coast necklace and earrings

This necklace and its matching earrings were inspired by the seashores near my home in the UK, a World Heritage Site famous for its fossils and geology. Learn about magical crimping to give a neat finish.

**See it GROW**

## NECKLACE

**STAGE 1** Make eight shell dangles by threading A, B, and C onto a headpin and making a wire-wrapped loop (see page 24). Trim the ends. Make one longer dangle by adding a D and an extra B at the top of the dangle.

**STAGE 2** Cut approximately 15" (38cm) of beading wire and put a bead stopper or paper clip on one end. String [B, E, B, F, C, shell dangle, C, F] four times. Make sure all the ammonites are facing the same way.

**STAGE 3** String a C, the longer dangle, and another C. This is the center of the necklace.

**STAGE 4** Reverse the stringing sequence from Stage 2 for the other half of the necklace. Remember to string the ammonites facing the other way.

STAGE 1

C →
B →
A →

Wrapped-loop shell dangles x 8

Long dangle x 1

Note that the tiny beads on either side of the wire-wrapped dangles are essential to the success of this design: without them, the dangles won't hang freely and the whole thing will be too stiff. Use 11º seed beads if you don't have 2mm silver rounds.

B   E        F   C

STAGE 2

STAGE 2

STAGE 3

The longer dangle is the center of the necklace.

**STAGE 5** Add a 2mm crimp tube and a seed bead. Pass the wire through a 7mm soldered jump ring and back through the seed bead, the crimp, and a few more beads. Use magical pliers to turn the crimp into a nice round bead shape (see page 42). Trim the spare wire. Remove the bead stopper or paper clip and repeat the crimping at the other end of the necklace.

STAGE 4

**Tip** **Adapt and rearrange** You could make this necklace more random by using a wider variety of beach-themed beads. Pearls would add a touch of glamor; the silver components could be replaced by bronze or copper for added warmth.

STAGE 5

Continued next page

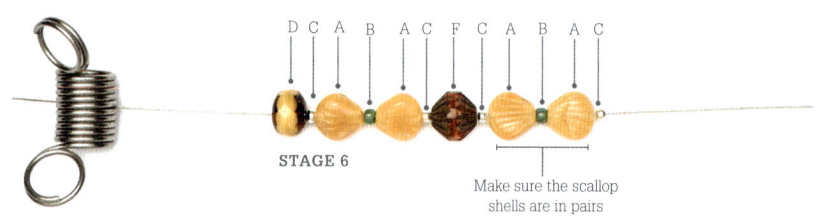

D C A B A C F C A B A C

**STAGE 6**

Make sure the scallop shells are in pairs facing outward.

**STAGE 6** For the second strand, cut approximately 13" (33cm) of beading wire and put a bead stopper or paper clip on one end. String [D, C, A, B, A, C, F, C, A, B, A, C] twice. Make sure the scallop shells are in pairs facing outward.

**STAGE 7**

String Stage 6 twice.

**STAGE 8**

**STAGE 7** String D, C, A, B, F—the bicone is the center bead. Reverse the entire sequence for the second half of the strand.

**STAGE 8** Add a seed bead, crimp, and seed bead at each end of the strand. Crimp to the same soldered rings as the ends of the first strand.

**STAGE 9** For the short back strands, cut two pieces of beading wire approximately 5" (12.5cm) long. String beads as shown in the photos or until the beadwork is approximately 4" (10cm) long. Finish with B, crimp tube, B. Crimp each strand to one of the soldered rings, so each ring has three strands attached.

**STAGE 10** Finish the other end of each short strand with a good bead, crimp, and seed bead and add a wire guardian before crimping. Use 6mm open jump rings to attach the clasp to one end and the remaining soldered ring to the other (see page 23).

**STAGE 9**

Each ring should have three strands attached.

**STAGE 10**

## TECHNIQUE: MAGICAL CRIMPING

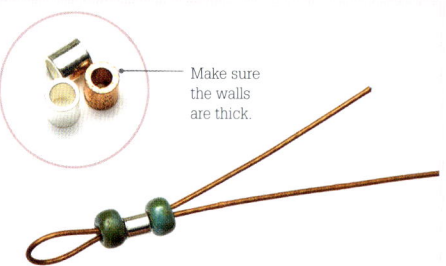

Make sure the walls are thick.

**STEP 1**
Make sure the last one or two beads of your strand have holes big enough to take a double thickness of beading wire. Note that magical crimping pliers will ONLY work with the correct thickness of beading wire, so make sure you have the right size of pliers for the thickness of your wire.

**STEP 2**
At the end of your beads, string a 2 x 2mm crimp tube. Add another bead and a wire guardian if you are using one. Thread the end of the wire back through the last bead and the crimp.

**STEP 3**
Position the crimp in the hollow in the plier jaws as shown, and squash gently until the jaws are fully closed.

## DESIGNING WITH A BEAD BOARD

A bead board (see page 21) is useful for designing multistrand necklaces like this one. You can lay out and arrange your feature beads, and when constructing the necklace you can keep all the components in the right places on the bead board to make the final assembly quick and easy.

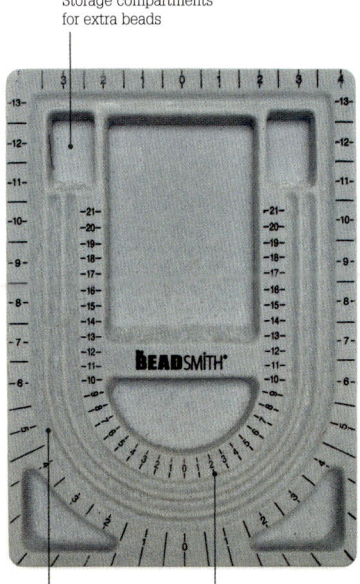

Storage compartments for extra beads

BEADSMITH®

Grooves to hold up to three rows of beads

Measurements to show you how long the rows will be

**See it GROW**

## EARRINGS

x 2

**STAGE 1** Make two wrapped-loop dangles with the eyepins and ammonite beads. Make sure the wrapped loop is at right angles to the eyepin loop. Attach each one to an earwire.

x 2

**STAGE 2** Make three pairs of wrapped-loop dangles with the remaining headpins, accent beads, seed beads, and silver rounds.

**STAGE 3** Open the remaining jump rings and attach three headpin dangles to each one, with the longest dangle in the center.

**STAGE 4** Attach the jump rings to the bottom loops of the eyepins, making sure the dangle clusters are mirror images of each other.

Should look like a ravioli package

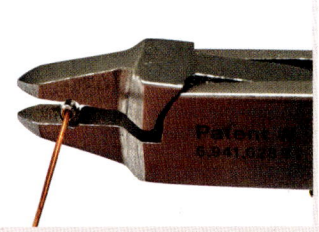

**STEP 4**
You should now have something that looks like a little square ravioli package with four flat corners. Turn it through 90 degrees and put it back in the pliers.

**STEP 5**
Squash the crimp again. Rotate it a little way and close the pliers again. Keep doing this until the pliers close fully all the way around the crimp. The crimp is now transformed into a neat little round bead shape. No sharp ends, no need for a crimp cover. Magic!

Pull the end until most of the slack has been taken up.

**STEP 6**
Repeat at the other end of your bead strand. To tension correctly before fixing the crimp, pick the strand up by the uncrimped end and hold the loop of wire, pulling the end with your other hand until most of the slack has been taken up. This takes a little practice but will soon become second nature.

# Strandline bracelet

Like sparkling sea-washed treasures from a tropical beach, glossy glass beads and pearls are teamed with crystals and plenty of silver in this elegant, delicate bracelet. Spacer bars keep the two strands just the right distance apart, and a filigree clasp is the perfect finishing touch.

### ZIGZAG PATTERN

This project is great for using up a few pairs of random accent beads. You don't have to go for a formal pattern; as long as the total length of each section is the same, the bars will still lie straight. It takes a little more ingenuity to fix it so that the beads form a zigzag pattern, but it can be done, so have fun experimenting!

## YOU WILL NEED

### BEAD BOX

- 24 cream opal 8º seed beads (A)
- 40 puce glow 11º seed beads (B)
- 10 ivory 12mm 2-hole glass divider bars (C)
- 6 pale pink 4mm freshwater pearls (D)
- 24 silver 2mm round beads (E)
- 12 silver 4 x 5mm flower spacers (F)
- 4 golden shadow 6 x 4mm crystal faceted rondelles (G)
- 8 carnelian pink 6mm glass rondelles (H)
- 2 caramel 9mm glass scallop beads (I)
- 4 golden shadow 4mm crystal bicones (J)
- 2 pale green 9 x 4mm lampwork glass spacers (K)
- 1 silver 10mm heart charm

### HARDWARE

- .018" (.46mm) flexible beading wire
- 4 silver 2 x 2mm crimp tubes
- 4 silver 4mm fine-gauge jump rings
- 1 silver 14 x 9mm 2-strand box clasp
- 1 silver 6mm jump ring

### TOOLKIT

- Diagonal wire cutters
- Bead stopper or paper clip
- Flat-nosed pliers (2 pairs)
- Magical crimping pliers

**Finished bracelet:** Approximately 8" (20cm) long

See it GROW

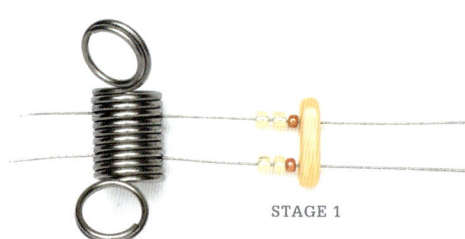

STAGE 1

**STAGE 1** Cut two pieces of flexible beading wire approximately 11" (28cm) long. Attach both to the same bead stopper, about ½" (1.2cm) apart. String two As and one B on each wire. String one hole of a C onto each wire.

STAGE 2

**STAGE 2** String B, D, B on each wire. Add another C.

STAGE 3

**STAGE 3** String B, E, F, E, G, A, B on one wire, and B, E, F, E, two Hs, B on the other. The two sections should be equal in length. Add another C.

STAGE 4

**STAGE 4** Repeat the Stage 3 sequences of beads in reverse, stringing them on opposite wires (refer to the photograph). Add another C.

STAGE 5

**STAGE 5** Add B, I, B to one wire and B, two As, D, B to the other. Add another C.

**STAGE 6** String the center section B, E, F, E, J, K, J, two As, E, F, E, B on each wire, reversing the sequence of beads on the second wire. Add another C.

STAGE 6

Try to pick pairs of pearls that are the same size.

STAGE 7

String both strands together and make sure that each divider bar lies straight when you add it. If it's crooked, that probably means you've left out a bead somewhere.

**STAGE 7** Mirror the first half of the bracelet, stringing the sequences on opposite wires as well as in reverse (see the photograph). Add or subtract beads at the ends to reach the required length, remembering to allow 1" (2.5cm) for the clasp.

**STAGE 8** Finish each of the four ends with a crimp and an A bead. Pass the wire back through the last few beads, secure the crimp (see page 42), and trim the wire ends.

**STAGE 9** Use the 4mm jump rings to attach one loop of the clasp to each wire end (see page 23). Use the 6mm ring to attach the charm to one of the 4mm jump rings.

Use magical crimping pliers to secure the crimp.

STAGE 8

STAGE 9

**Tip Two-part clasps**
Attach two-part clasps with the clasp fastened, to ensure you fix both halves the right way up.

## YOU WILL NEED

**BEAD BOX**

- 4 beige 10mm coin pearls
- 14 assorted pink, white, and brown 3-5mm freshwater pearls
- 4 caramel 9mm pressed glass scallop beads
- 18 mixed 4mm ocean jasper rounds
- 4 pink and/or white 8º glass seed beads
- 22 silver 11º metal seed beads
- 10 silver 4mm metal star charms
- 2 silver 10mm metal heart charms

**HARDWARE**

- 22" (55cm) of medium silver curb chain (link size up to approximately 5 x 3mm and they must be open links, not soldered–you should be able to open and close the links with pliers)
- 2 silver 2" (5cm) eyepins
- 2 silver bead cones
- Pair of silver earwires
- 22 silver 1" (2.5cm) fine-gauge headpins

**TOOLKIT**

- Flat-nosed pliers (two pairs)
- Diagonal wire cutters
- Round-nosed pliers
- One-step looper tool (optional)

**Finished earrings:** Approximately 4½" (11cm) long, excluding earwires

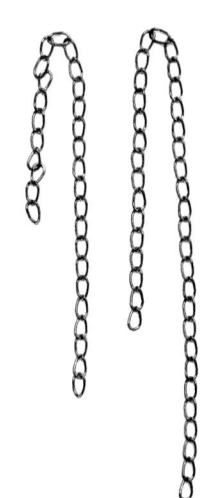

**STAGE 1** Use two pairs of flat-nosed pliers to open links in the chain in the same way as you would open a jump ring (see page 23) so as to divide it into two 6" (15cm) and two 5" (12.5cm) lengths.

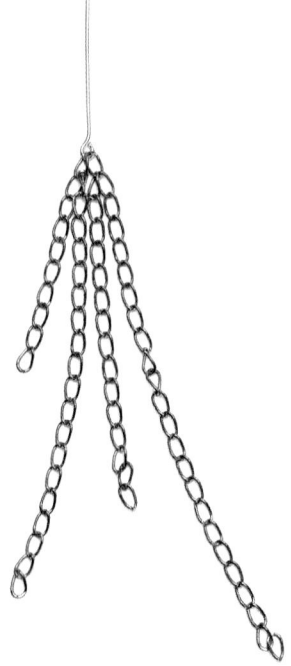

**STAGE 2** Take a 6" (15cm) and a 5" (12.5cm) length and fold them in two, so that each of the four ends is a slightly different length. The longest should be approximately 3½" (9cm). Use flat-nosed pliers to open the loop of an eyepin and attach it to the link where each chain folds. Close the loop.

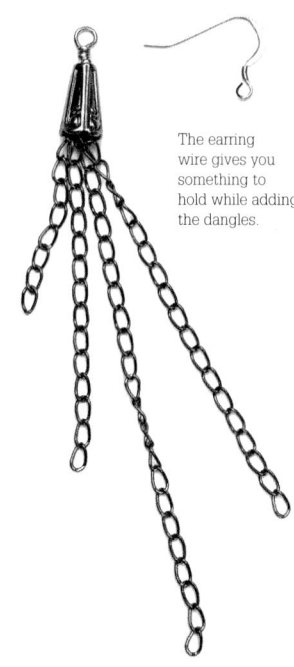

The earring wire gives you something to hold while adding the dangles.

**STAGE 3** String a bead cone and a metal seed bead onto the eyepin and form a wire-wrapped loop (see page 24) at the top. Trim the end of the wire close to the wrapped coil. Open the loop of an earwire and attach it to the wrapped loop. Make a second earring in the same way.

# Summer nights earrings

Nighttimes on the beach: The wet sand gleams in the moonlight, stars twinkle in the sky, and love is in the air. This casual, summery earring design is the perfect thing to wear to a barefoot beach party. Add simple charms and pearly dangles to a cascade of chains, all held together with a silvery bead cone and some wire wrapping.

**STAGE 4** Make bead and pearl dangles on all the headpins. String a bead or pearl, a jasper round or 8º seed bead, and a metal seed bead.

**STAGE 5** Form a simple loop in each headpin using pliers or a one-step looper (see page 22) and trim the end if necessary. Divide the dangles into two equal groups.

STAGE 6

STAGE 7

**STAGE 6** Starting at the top, and with the largest dangles, open the loop on each dangle in turn and attach it to a link in the chain tassel. It's easiest if you hold the earwire and let the chain hang down so you can see how the dangles will hang.

**STAGE 7** Add 11 dangles to each chain tassel, rearranging until you're happy with their appearance.

**STAGE 8** Open the sixth link from the end of the longest chain and attach a star charm (see page 23). Do the same three links from the end. Add a heart charm to the end link of the longest chain, and star charms to the ends of the other three chains. Repeat Stages 5–8 on the second earring.

This design lends itself to experimentation. Make the chains shorter (or even longer!), use copper or gold metal rather than silver, add crystals, or use a big bead in place of the bead cone.

**Tips Bead shapes** Do bear in mind that the shape of the beads you use is important. If you choose beads larger than about 5mm in diameter, make sure they are flattened or drop shapes rather than round. Big round beads will push the chain out of shape and it won't hang in an elegant tassel any more. Flat beads will overlap and allow the chain to hang freely.

**Soldered links** If you find you only have chain with soldered links, don't worry–you can still make this design. Just find some small (3-4mm) jump rings and use those to attach the charms to the chain, instead of adding them to the links directly.

# Perfect pearl necklace

Pearls are traditionally strung on silk with tiny knots tied in between each one. The knots keep the pearls separate so they can't rub together and damage the beautiful luster. A knotted necklace has the added advantage that if it should break you will lose at most one pearl.

## YOU WILL NEED

**BEAD BOX**
- 2 11º seed beads
- 27 ocean jasper
  4 x 2mm rondelles
- 25 cocoa 10mm coin pearls

**HARDWARE**
- 1 card .5mm (No. 3) silk bead stringing cord with needle
- 2 silver 4mm clamshell bead tips (calotte crimps)
- 2 silver 4mm jump rings
- 1 silver 10mm lobster claw clasp
- 1 silver 6mm soldered (closed) jump ring

**TOOLKIT**
- Flat-nosed pliers (2 pairs)
- Sharp scissors
- Pearl knotting tool
- E-6000 glue (optional)

**Finished necklace:**
Approximately 18" (45cm) long

**See it GROW**

**STAGE 1** Unwind all of the silk cord from the card and pull hard on it to take the kinks out. String one seed bead and pull most of the silk through it; tie an overhand knot around it (see page 22), leaving a 3" (7.5cm) tail. Tie a second knot in the same place.

**STAGE 2** String a clamshell bead tip and position the seed bead and knots inside the "shell" portion.

STAGE 1

STAGE 2

Position the seed bead and two knots inside the "shell" of the bead tip.

## TECHNIQUE: PEARL KNOTTING WITH A KNOTTING TOOL

**STEP 1**
String all of the pearls and/or beads required for your necklace. Slide the first pearl to the end of the silk, next to the clasp you've attached.

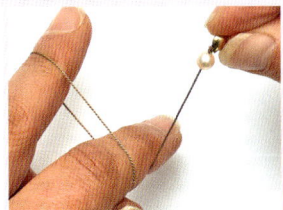

**STEP 2**
Hold the end with the pearl in your right hand and wrap the silk around two spread fingers of your left hand, as shown. The silk will form a loop.

**STEP 3**
Pass the pearl and the clasp through the loop from left to right, making a loose knot around your fingers. Study the photograph above and make sure the thread is aligned as shown.

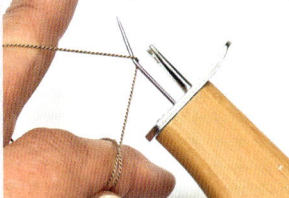

**STEP 4**
Let go of the pearl and pick up the knotting tool. Insert the needle part of the tool into the loop of the knot from left to right. Take your fingers out of the loop and pull the thread gently to tighten the knot.

**STAGE 3** Use flat-nosed pliers to squeeze the clamshell shut, enclosing the seed bead and trapping the end of the silk. Trim the loose short end.

**STAGE 4** Use the pearl knotting tool (see Technique) to tie a knot next to the bead tip.

**STAGE 5** String a jasper rondelle onto the thread. Slide it along until it rests against the first knot you tied.

**STAGE 6** Now use the pearl knotting tool to tie another knot above the jasper bead. String a pearl and slide it down to rest against the knot you just tied. Tie another knot after the pearl. Continue in this way, alternating jasper and pearls, until all the beads are knotted together.

**STAGE 7** String the other clamshell bead tip and seed bead. Slide them down the thread until they rest against the last knot. Tie an overhand knot around the seed bead; insert the tip of the knotting-tool needle into the loop and pull it down the thread as far as you can, then tie a second knot around the bead.

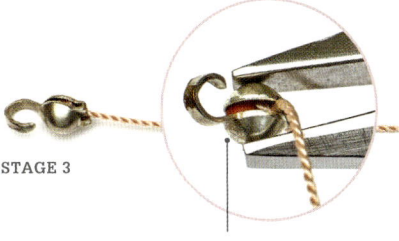

STAGE 3

For extra security, add a drop of E-6000 glue to the knots and allow to dry before closing the clamshell.

STAGE 4

STAGE 5

STAGE 6

**Tip Take care** Don't pull the knots too tight, since by doing so you risk breaking the thread. You'll soon get a feel for when to stop.

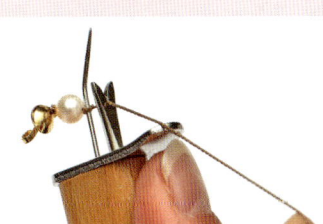

STAGE 7

**Tip Improvise** If you don't have a pearl knotting tool, you can use a large needle or an awl instead. Put the point of the needle through the loop of the knot, and move the knot down the thread until it lies against the last pearl.

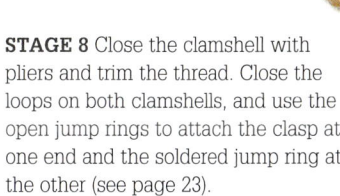

STAGE 8

**STAGE 8** Close the clamshell with pliers and trim the thread. Close the loops on both clamshells, and use the open jump rings to attach the clasp at one end and the soldered jump ring at the other (see page 23).

**STEP 5**
When the knot is tightened around the needle, use the tool to move the knot down the thread until the knot is next to your first pearl. Insert the thread into the Y-shaped part of the tool and pull.

**STEP 6**
Push upward with your right thumb, holding the silk taut with your left hand, until the knot pops off the tip of the needle.

**STEP 7**
You should now have a perfectly tied knot next to your first pearl.

**STEP 8**
Slide your next pearl down the silk to rest against the knot you just tied. Repeat from Step 2 until your knotted strand is the desired length. Finish the strand according to the project instructions.

## YOU WILL NEED

**BEAD BOX**

- 30 (approx.) mixed pastel 6-10mm glass accent beads (flowers, leaves, butterflies, hearts, or whatever else takes your fancy)
- 30 (approx.) mixed 3-4mm accent beads (rondelles, flower spacers, cubes, hearts, or similar)
- 30 (approx.) mixed 6º seed beads and/or triangle beads
- 21 (approx.) mixed 4mm Japanese fringe drops
- A pinch of 11º seed beads
- 50 (approx.) yellow brass 11º metal seed beads
- 2 8º seed beads
- 1 floral 18mm glass button with shank

**HARDWARE**

- .018" (.46mm) flexible beading wire
- 2 silver 2 x 2mm crimp tubes
- 1 brass or gold 6mm jump ring

**TOOLKIT**

- Diagonal wire cutters
- Bead stopper or paper clip
- Flat-nosed pliers (2 pairs)
- Magical crimping pliers

**Finished bracelet:** Approximately 24" (60cm) long, which will wrap three times around a 7¹/₂" (19cm) wrist

# Wildflower wrap bracelet

Simple techniques are all you need to transform a handful of beads into this pretty, springtime wrap bracelet that doubles as a necklace. A floral button features as the clasp. As an alternative, you could reuse a vintage treasure from your button box.

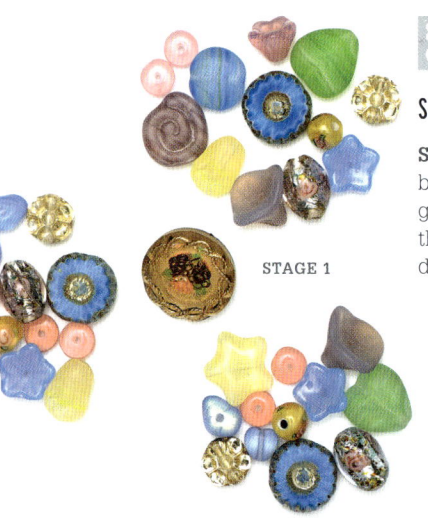

**See it GROW**

### STRINGING THE BRACELET

**STAGE 1** Divide your accent beads into three roughly equal groups, which will ensure that the colors and shapes are distributed evenly.

**STAGE 1**

**Tip Color checking** Before stringing, mix your beads together and take a good look at the color mix, to make sure it is harmonious. Sometimes one particular color stands out and doesn't quite fit in with the rest. In that case, take it out and substitute something else. If you're not confident about mixing colors, go for a simple approach such as black and white, or shades of blue.

STAGE 2

String a 11º seed bead between each accent bead.

STAGE 3

String rondelles in pairs.

String drops in threes.

**STAGE 2** Cut a piece of flexible beading wire about 30" (90cm) long and put a bead stopper or paper clip on the end. Start stringing beads, alternating larger and smaller accent beads and putting a 11º seed bead between each one. String rondelles and flower spacers in pairs, and drops in threes.

**STAGE 3** Continue to string until the first group of accents is used up.

**STAGE 4** String the second group of accents and as many of the third as you need to make a strand that will wrap around your wrist three times—remember, the clasp will add another 1½" (4cm) so you may not need all the beads.

STAGE 4

## MAKING THE BUTTON AND LOOP CLASP

**STAGE 5** Make the button end of the clasp first. Finish the strand with a crimp tube, a 8º seed bead, and 8 metal seed beads. Go back through the 8º seed bead, the crimp, and a few more beads. Pull the little loop snug, secure the crimp (see page 22), and trim the end of the wire.

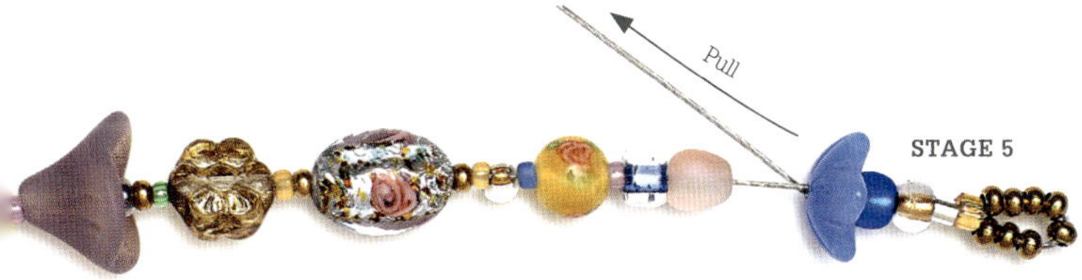

*Pull*

STAGE 5

**STAGE 6** Use pliers and the jump ring to attach the button shank to the beadwork (see page 23).

Open the jump ring and use it to attach the button shank to the beadwork.

STAGE 6

**STAGE 7** Remove the bead stopper or paper clip from the other end of the wire. String a crimp tube, a 8º seed bead, and 30 metal seed beads, or enough to make a loop that fits over your button. Go back through the 8º bead, the crimp, and a few more beads. Check the fit before securing the crimp and trimming the end of the wire.

**Tip Think comfort** This project gives you a lot of scope for your own design choices, and is a lovely way to use small numbers of pretty beads. Have fun raiding your bead boxes to see what you can find. Just make sure there are no spiky corners that might be uncomfortable.

STAGE 7

## YOU WILL NEED

### BEAD BOX

- 8 purple transparent 4 x 6mm glass bellflowers
- 13 mauve opaque 8º Japanese seed beads
- 5g (approx.) light orange opaque 11º Czech seed beads
- 1g (approx.) mauve opaque 11º Czech seed beads
- 5 sunflower yellow Picasso 12mm square table-cut flower beads
- 1 yellow and purple 1" (25mm) artisan lampwork glass toggle clasp with integral jump rings

### HARDWARE

- .018" (.46mm) satin copper finish flexible beading wire
- 6 copper 2 x 2mm crimp tubes
- 2 copper 2" (50mm) eyepins
- 2 copper 12 x 10mm leaf-patterned end cones
- 3 copper 6mm jump rings
- 5 copper 2" (50mm) headpins

### TOOLKIT

- Diagonal wire cutters
- At least 3 bead stoppers or paper clips
- Bead spinner (optional)
- Flat-nosed pliers (2 pairs)

Learn how to turn simple beaded strands into a tactile, flexible braided bracelet in bright sunshine colors that will cheer up even the grayest of days. You'll want to wear this little piece of summertime all year round!

# Marigold bracelet

**STAGE 1**

**STAGE 2**

## STRINGING THE BRACELET

**STAGE 1** Cut six pieces of beading wire approximately 9" (23cm) long. Take two pieces and string a bellflower, a 8º seed bead, and a crimp tube onto both wires together, pulling about 1" (2.5cm) of wire through the beads (A). Pass the short end back through the crimp and the seed bead (B). Crush the crimp with flat-nosed pliers (see Tips) and trim the short end (C). Repeat with the other two pairs of wires.

**STAGE 2** String a random mix of 11º seed beads onto each wire separately until each beaded strand is approximately 7" (17cm) long. If you have a bead spinner, use this to mix up the beads. Secure the loose ends with bead stoppers or paper clips.

## TECHNIQUE: BRAIDING

**STEP 1**
Working away from you, separate the three (in this case double) strands of beads.

**STEP 2**
Bring the right-hand strand over to the center. Then bring the left-hand strand to the center. Do not allow the two parts of the strand to twist: keep them side by side at all times.

**STEP 3**
Bring the right-hand strand to the center again. Make sure the braid is still heading straight away from you and that your slack (bare wire) is at the far end of all the strands.

**STEP 4**
Keep bringing alternate side strands to the center until you have braided all the beads. Try to keep the angle of each crossover the same; this will get harder toward the end of the braid as the beadwork gets stiffer. Once the ends are secured, work the braid with your fingers to even it up.

STAGE 3

Allow 3–4mm slack.

STAGE 4

Hook one end of each pair into the loop of an eyepin.

STAGE 5

STAGE 6

STAGE 7

**STAGE 3** Make sure all the pairs of strands are the same length. On each pair in turn, string a bellflower, seed bead, and crimp tube. Secure as you did in Stage 1. It is important to allow ⅛" (3–4mm) of slack in the wire, otherwise it will be too stiff to braid.

**STAGE 4** Open the loop of an eyepin with pliers and hook one end of each pair into it. Close the loop. String an end cone and a 8° bead and make a wire-wrapped loop (see page 24).

**STAGE 5** Braid the paired strands together (see Technique).

**STAGE 6** Attach the three ends to the other eyepin and finish with an end cone and a wrapped loop, as in Stage 4.

**STAGE 7** Use two pairs of pliers to attach one half of the clasp to each end. Attach the toggle with an extra jump ring to ensure it has room to go through the glass loop.

## MAKING AND ADDING THE DANGLES

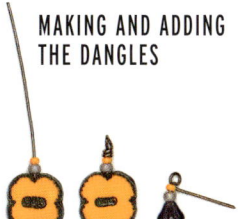

**STAGE 8** Make five wrapped-loop dangles with the sunflowers and remaining bellflowers on headpins.

Add dangles to the center of the braid.

**STAGE 9** Add two dangles to the center of the braid with a jump ring (see page 23). Add the remaining dangles to the first ring attaching the toggle clasp.

**Tips Simple crimping** Do not use crimping pliers for this project. With four thicknesses of wire going through the crimp, the pliers will not work effectively. Simply flatten the crimps with flat-nosed pliers. The crimps will be hidden by the end cones, in any case.

**Contrast color** The main color used here is golden-orange, and its warmth goes well with antiqued copper findings. Purple is the "opposite" of orange on the color wheel and provides a vibrant contrast. The trick is not to use too much purple: a little here and there is enough.

**Alternative colorways** This design would lend itself well to all kinds of other color combinations. Why not find an artisan glass clasp you really love, and use it as a basis for your palette? Or try an ethnic look with turquoise, coral, and silver? You could also add more charms along the length for a fuller texture, or make each bead strand a different color.

**Finished bracelet:** Approximately 8½" (22cm) long

## YOU WILL NEED

### BEAD BOX
- 25 (approx.) purple 8º Japanese seed beads
- 30 (approx.) brass 11º metal seed beads
- 15 (approx.) purple 6º seed beads
- 24 assorted 4-12mm accent beads, such as hearts, daisies, and bellflowers, preferably in multiples of 4
- 20 apollo gold 8 x 4mm side-drilled 6-petal glass flowers
- 36 jonquil matte AB 5mm glass flower spacers
- 16 pink opaque 4mm glass rondelles
- 12 peridot 3mm glass rondelles
- 16 raw brass 8mm fancy flower mini-drop charms
- 16 raw brass 5mm fancy heart mini-drop charms

### HARDWARE
- 6' (2m) light green medium pearl stringing silk with wire needle
- 2" (50mm) gold or brass French (bullion) wire cut into 8 equal pieces
- 8 gold 6mm jump rings
- 16 gold 4mm jump rings

### TOOLKIT
- Diagonal wire cutters
- Pearl knotting tool (or a sharp awl and a pair of tweezers)
- Sharp scissors
- Flat-nosed pliers (2 pairs)
- E-6000 glue (optional)
- Toothpick or cocktail stick (if using glue)

**Finished necklace:**
Approximately 28" (70cm) long

# Nostalgia necklace

A modern twist on vintage techniques, this project uses two very traditional methods, knotting and French (bullion) wire, to create a long necklace with lots of pretty glass flower beads and clusters of gently tinkling charms. The perfect accessory for a summer's day!

 **See it GROW**

**STAGE 1** Divide your beads into four roughly equal groups. Follow Steps 1–4 of the Technique, below, to start your first section with a loop of French (bullion) wire. Start threading the rest of the beads from the first group.

STAGE 1

## TECHNIQUE: STARTING AND FINISHING WITH FRENCH (BULLION) WIRE

**STEP 1**
Unwind all of the silk from the card and straighten the needle as much as possible. Pull on the silk to remove at least some of the kinks. String the first 2-3 beads in reverse order, then 3 8º seed beads. Slide them to within 2" (5cm) of the end of the silk.

**STEP 2**
Thread a piece of French (bullion) wire onto the needle and very carefully slide it down the silk until it rests against the beads.

**STEP 3**
Thread the needle back through the end bead and pull gently until all the silk is through the bead and the French (bullion) wire forms a U-shape. Knot the thread around itself. Work slowly and carefully and don't pull the knot too tight.

**STAGE 2** Knot between each bead or short set of beads (see Technique, page 48). Follow the photograph, or make up your own pattern. If a bead (e.g., a 6º bead) has a large hole, put a small seed bead before and after it.

← Knot between each bead or short set of beads.

**STAGE 3** When you are halfway through the section, add a jump ring to the next knot.

**STAGE 4** Use the jump ring to pull the knot snugly against the previous bead. Continue knotting with your knotting tool until you are 4 or 5 beads from the end. Finish with French (bullion) wire (see Steps 5–6, below). Make three more knotted sections in the same way. Trim all of the silk ends very carefully close to the beads.

**STAGE 5** Use pliers to put a brass flower or heart charm onto a 4mm jump ring (see page 23). Close the jump ring.

**STAGE 6** Open another jump ring. Put on a brass charm, the jump ring from Stage 6, and another brass charm, then close the ring. Make a total of eight charm clusters in the same way, choosing hearts or flowers at random.

**STAGE 7** Add a cluster plus a single brass charm to each of the jump rings knotted into the silk. Use the remaining 6mm jump rings to join the sections together, adding a cluster and a single charm as you do so.

**Tip** **Take care with French (bullion) wire** French (bullion) wire is a coil of very fine wire that protects the ends of your thread. Handle with extreme care and never, ever, pull or twist it, since it comes unraveled very easily and is impossible to reshape. Cut it with your sharpest diagonal wire cutters.

Make eight charm clusters.

STAGE 5

STAGE 6

STAGE 7

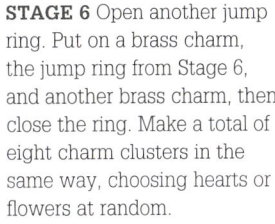

For extra security, add a drop of glue to each of the three knots at the ends of each section. Leave to dry thoroughly, preferably overnight.

**STEP 4**
Thread the needle back through the next bead and tie another knot. You can pull this knot a little tighter. Go back through the third bead and knot a third time. Go back through all the remaining beads, then continue with threading and knotting as described in your project.

**STEP 5**
Finish the strand with 2–3 beads, 3 flower spacers, and another piece of French (bullion) wire. Leave a millimeter or two of slack, no more.

**STEP 6**
Go back through the flower spacers one at a time, tying a knot between each one. Thread the needle carefully back through the next 2–3 beads and cut off the surplus silk, leaving an inch or so attached to the beadwork (you will trim all these ends later; see Stage 4, above).

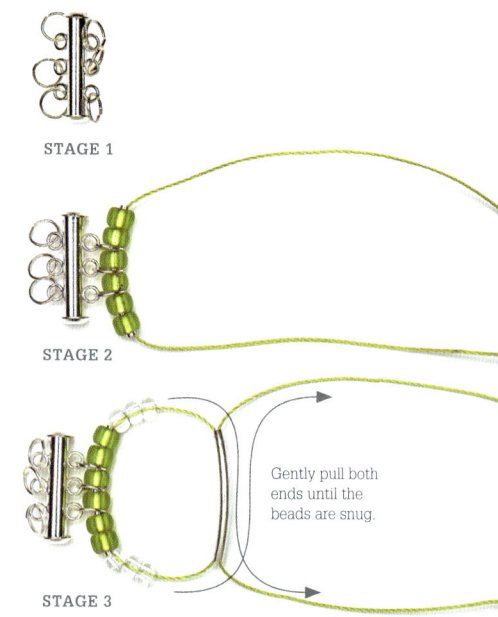

# Sunny morning bracelet

Imagine a meadow when the sun is shining, birds are singing, a butterfly visits the flowers, and all the colors are fresh and sparkling with dew. A few simple techniques are all you need to create this cheery, bright bracelet, and enjoy the pretty tinkling sounds it makes.

## YOU WILL NEED

### BEAD BOX
- 18–20 silver 2 x 25mm curved tube or "noodle" beads
- 21–25 lime green "E" beads or 6mm pony beads, hole size bigger than 2mm
- 102–114 clear 6⁹ glass seed beads
- 8–10 silver or pewter 6–20mm charms with hanging loops
- 13–15 assorted 6–12mm lampwork glass spacer beads, pony beads, and/or metal beads, all with hole size bigger than 2mm

### HARDWARE
- 6 silver 6mm jump rings
- 1 silver 20mm 3-row sliding tube clasp
- 5' (1.5m) lime green C-Lon or other nylon macramé cord
- 8–10 silver 4mm jump rings

### TOOLKIT
- Flat-nosed pliers (2 pairs)
- Sharp scissors
- E-6000 glue (optional)

**Finished bracelet:** Approximately 8" (20cm) long by 1¹⁄₄" (30mm) wide

**See it GROW**

**STAGE 1** Use flat-nosed pliers to attach a 6mm jump ring to each of the rings on the sliding tube clasp (see page 23).

**STAGE 2** String a tube bead onto the C-Lon or nylon cord. String two E beads, then alternate 6mm jump rings (with clasp attached) and E beads, then a final two E beads. Make sure the E beads go over the tube. Slide the whole assembly to the center of the cord.

**STAGE 3** On one end of the cord, string three clear beads. On the other end, string three clear beads and a tube. Put the first end of the cord through the tube in the opposite direction. Pull both ends gently until the beads are snug together.

**STAGE 1**

**STAGE 2**

**STAGE 3**

Gently pull both ends until the beads are snug.

**STAGE 4** Repeat Stage 3, adding a charm between the clear beads (use a 4mm jump ring to attach it if the hanging loop is not at right angles to the charm). Add one or two spacer, pony, or metal beads to the tube before you put the thread through it.

**STAGE 5** Continue linking tubes, adding beads at random as you go. Put 5 E beads on one or two links. Use 4mm jump rings to attach charms to either the tubes or the clear edge beads. Use all but one of the tubes.

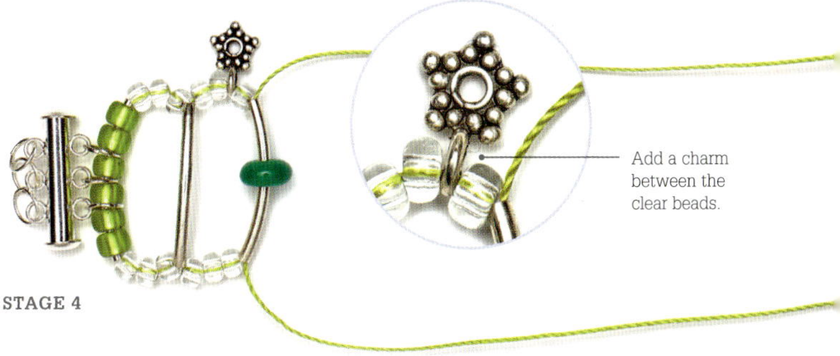

Attach a charm to a tube.

STAGE 4

Add a charm between the clear beads.

STAGE 5

STAGE 6

**STAGE 6** Check the length, allowing 1" (2.5cm) for the clasp, and add or subtract tubes as necessary. Add the final tube, stringing beads and the rings attached to the clasp, as in Stage 2.

**STAGE 7** Weave one cord end back through the edge beads and the second tube from the end. Weave the other loose end back through the edge beads to meet it.

**STAGE 8** Knot the two ends together with a double overhand knot (see page 22), pulling tightly. Weave the ends through as many beads and tubes as possible, then trim the excess. Add a drop of glue to the knot if you like, for extra security.

STAGE 7

Knot the two ends together with a double overhand knot, pulling tightly.

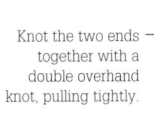

STAGE 8

**Tips** **Bangle variation** You can make this as a seamless bangle by leaving out the clasp and weaving through the first tube instead of adding a separate last one. You might need to add an extra tube or two to make it long enough to fit over your hand.

**Adjust the construction** Experiment with different beads for the ladder construction. For example, you could use seed beads in place of the tubes. You might need a needle on your thread if the beads you pick are very small, but the construction is the same. Go wild, have fun, and don't be afraid to ask "What if...?" Beads can be recycled, and thread is cheap!

## YOU WILL NEED

**BEAD BOX**

* 5 silver 4mm flower spacers (A)
* 5 pink opal 9mm bellflowers (B)
* 33 pale pink 3mm firepolished rounds (C)
* 90 silver 2mm rounds (D)
* 34 pale green 4mm firepolished rounds (E)
* 12 pale green 7 x 4mm glass "Smartie" side-drilled disks (F)
* 10 pale yellow 4mm firepolished rounds (G)
* 50 clear multicolor 6mm "art glass" top-drilled flowers (H)
* 32 sapphire blue 4mm firepolished rounds (I)
* 6 grass green 4mm firepolished rounds (J)
* 10 sapphire blue 6mm bellflowers (K)
* 36 clear multicolor 16mm "art glass" daggers (L)
* 20 pink opal 4mm glass druks (M)
* 10 pale green 6mm firepolished rounds (N)

**HARDWARE**

* 5 silver 1" (25mm) headpins
* .018" (.46mm) flexible beading wire
* 10 silver 2 x 2mm crimp tubes
* 10 silver 4mm jump rings
* 2 antiqued pewter floral 3-to-1 connector links
* 1 silver 8mm round magnetic clasp (or clasp of your choice)

**TOOLKIT**

* Round-nosed pliers
* Flat-nosed pliers (2 pairs)
* Diagonal wire cutters
* Magical crimping pliers
* Bead stoppers or paper clips

**Finished necklace:** Approximately 23" (58cm) long

# English garden necklace

The delicate, pretty colors of an English country garden in spring are beautifully blended in this triple-strand necklace. Learn to mix and match your beads to give lots of visual interest in each part, while creating a harmonious whole.

Dangles x 5

**See it GROW**

**STAGE 1** String the following on each of the headpins: A, B, C, D. Make five wire-wrapped dangles (see Technique, page 24).

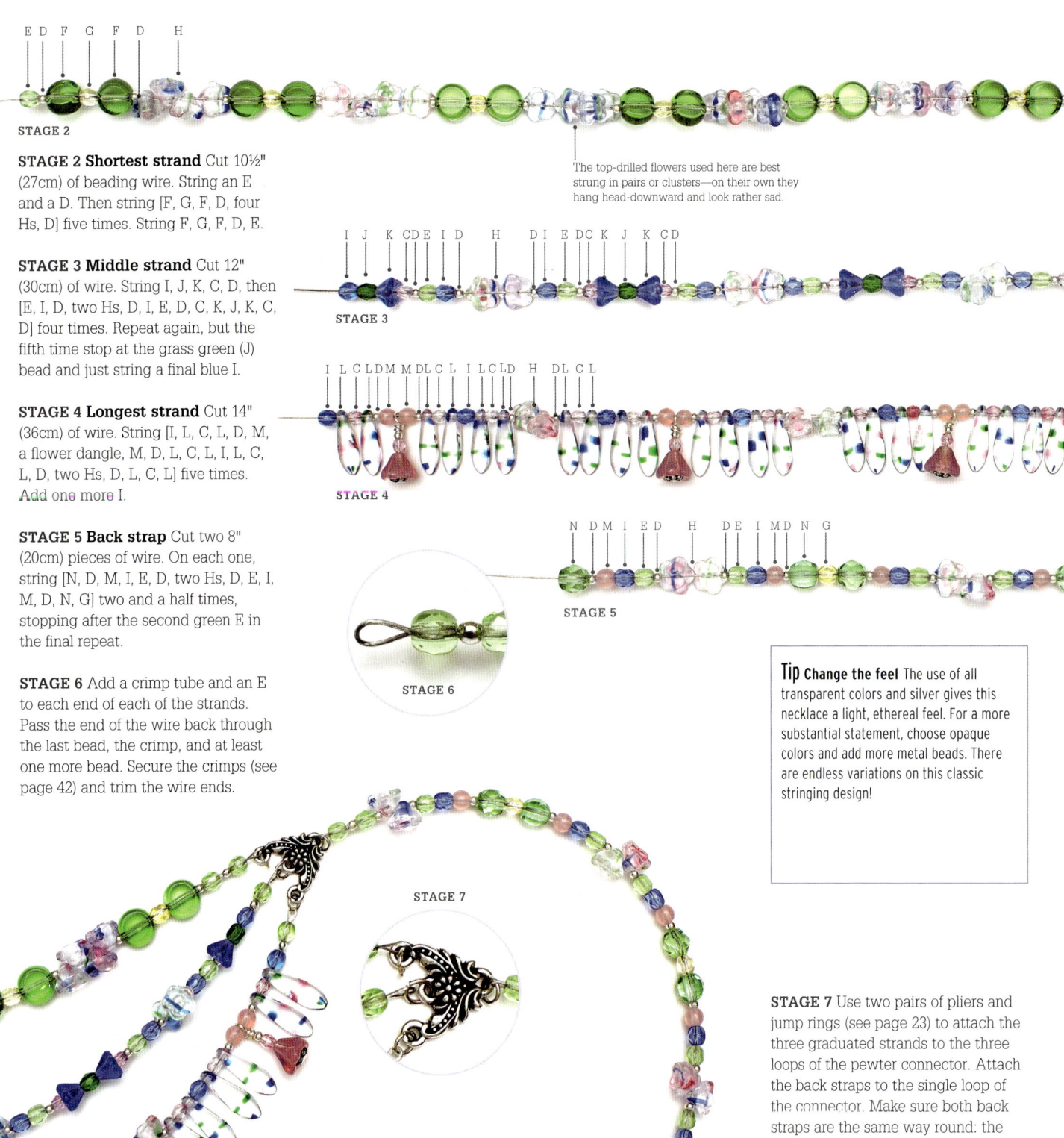

E D F G F D H

**STAGE 2**

**STAGE 2 Shortest strand** Cut 10½"
(27cm) of beading wire. String an E
and a D. Then string [F, G, F, D, four
Hs, D] five times. String F, G, F, D, E.

**STAGE 3 Middle strand** Cut 12"
(30cm) of wire. String I, J, K, C, D, then
[E, I, D, two Hs, D, I, E, D, C, K, J, K, C,
D] four times. Repeat again, but the
fifth time stop at the grass green (J)
bead and just string a final blue I.

**STAGE 4 Longest strand** Cut 14"
(36cm) of wire. String [I, L, C, L, D, M,
a flower dangle, M, D, L, C, L, I, L, C,
L, D, two Hs, D, L, C, L] five times.
Add one more I.

**STAGE 5 Back strap** Cut two 8"
(20cm) pieces of wire. On each one,
string [N, D, M, I, E, D, two Hs, D, E, I,
M, D, N, G] two and a half times,
stopping after the second green E in
the final repeat.

**STAGE 6** Add a crimp tube and an E
to each end of each of the strands.
Pass the end of the wire back through
the last bead, the crimp, and at least
one more bead. Secure the crimps (see
page 42) and trim the wire ends.

The top-drilled flowers used here are best
strung in pairs or clusters—on their own they
hang head-downward and look rather sad.

I J K CDE I D H D I E DC K J K C D

**STAGE 3**

I L C L D M M D L C L I L C L D H D L C L

**STAGE 4**

N D M I E D H D E I M D N G

**STAGE 5**

**STAGE 6**

**Tip Change the feel** The use of all
transparent colors and silver gives this
necklace a light, ethereal feel. For a more
substantial statement, choose opaque
colors and add more metal beads. There
are endless variations on this classic
stringing design!

**STAGE 7**

**STAGE 8**

**STAGE 7** Use two pairs of pliers and
jump rings (see page 23) to attach the
three graduated strands to the three
loops of the pewter connector. Attach
the back straps to the single loop of
the connector. Make sure both back
straps are the same way round: the
single N bead should be nearer to
the clasp.

**STAGE 8** Connect the clasp with the
final pair of jump rings.

This striking bracelet makes the most of a few special beads by framing them with bunches of tactile dangles. A single big heart adds the perfect finishing touch.

# Rustic romance bracelet

## YOU WILL NEED

**BEAD BOX**

- 45 assorted green, russet, and brown 4-6mm accent beads, such as crystals, rondelles, 6º seed beads, 8º triangles, and pressed glass hearts (A)
- 45 mixed green and brown 11º seed beads (B)
- 60 (approx.) copper 11º metal seed beads (C)
- 2 red 8º copper-lined Japanese triangle beads (D)
- 8 clear 6º copper-lined seed beads (E)
- 4 red transparent Picasso 16mm square window beads (F)
- 4 olive AB transparent 8mm square pressed glass tile beads (G)
- 1 red 18mm lampwork glass heart
- 1 Indian red 4mm crystal bicone

**HARDWARE**

- 45 copper 1" (25mm) headpins
- .018" (.46mm) flexible beading wire
- 2 silver 2 x 2mm crimp tubes
- 1 copper 2" (50mm) headpin
- 3 copper 4mm jump rings
- Copper toggle clasp

**TOOLKIT**

- Round-nosed pliers
- Flat-nosed pliers (2 pairs)
- Magical crimping pliers
- Diagonal wire cutters

**SEE IT GROW**

## STRINGING THE BRACELET

**STAGE 1** Use copper headpins to make 45 wrapped-loop dangles (see page 24) each with one A, one B, and finally one C bead.

STAGE 1

C
B
A

**STAGE 2** Divide the dangles into nine groups of five, distributing the colors and sizes roughly evenly between the groups.

STAGE 2

**STAGE 3** Cut 11" (28cm) of beading wire. String a crimp tube and a 8º triangle. Go back through the triangle and crimp, leaving a ½" (1.2cm) free end. Pull the long end of the wire until only a small loop shows above the triangle. Secure the crimp using magical crimping pliers (see Technique, page 42) until it forms a nice round bead shape. String [C, E, five dangles, F, five dangles, E, C, G]. Make sure the first few beads go over the short end of the wire so it's completely hidden.

E          F          G

STAGE 3

**Tip Change the mood** A simple change can make a big difference to this bracelet. Try it with silver findings to lighten the look, give it more impact with a simple black-and-white color scheme, or make it less rustic and more romantic with big pink hearts and clusters of flower dangles.

STAGE 4

**STAGE 4** Repeat the stringing sequence from Stage 3 three times. Check the bracelet fits, allowing for the size of the toggle, and add or subtract beads if necessary. String a metal seed bead, crimp, and a D bead. Go back through the D bead, the crimp, and a couple more beads. Pull all spare wire carefully through the beads, and secure the crimp.

## LAMPWORK HEART DANGLE

**STAGE 5** String the lampwork heart, 4mm crystal bicone, and a 6° seed bead on the 2" (50mm) headpin. The bicone fits into the top of the heart and helps to stabilize it on the wire.

STAGE 5

STAGE 6

**STAGE 6** You should have five wrapped-loop dangles left over from stringing the bracelet.

STAGE 7

**STAGE 7** Add these remaining dangles to the headpin, topped with a metal seed bead.

STAGE 8

**STAGE 8** Add a 6° seed bead and a metal seed bead to the headpin. Make a wrapped loop above the beads, as you did for the small dangles.

> **Tip Crimp with care**
> Be extra careful when securing the second crimp–it can be tricky to get the tension right with all those wrapped-loop dangles. Take your time and make sure the beads and wires are pushed nicely together so there won't be any bare wire showing.

**Finished bracelet:**
Approximately 8" (20cm) long

> **Tip Trouble-free toggles** Don't put the toggle part of your clasp right next to a big bead, or you won't be able to fasten it easily. Always allow a few small beads or an extra ring or two at the end of the bracelet, to make sure there is room to pull the toggle through the loop when fastening it.

## ASSEMBLY

**STAGE 9** Use two pairs of flat-nosed pliers to open all three jump rings (see page 23). Use one jump ring to attach the loop half of the toggle clasp to the start of the bracelet, and one to attach the toggle half to the other end. Use the third jump ring to attach the lampwork heart dangle to the jump ring next to the clasp loop.

# Fall leaves necklace

A new take on the traditional technique of French beading, where tiny seed beads are strung on wire to replicate leaves or petals.

## YOU WILL NEED

**BEAD BOX**
- 5g (approx.) total weight of 11º seed beads in five colors: terracotta, cream Ceylon, matte khaki, transparent amber, and chocolate brown
- 28 red jasper 4mm rounds
- 20 brown 9 x 6mm Picasso top-drilled pressed glass leaves

**HARDWARE**
- Gunmetal or bronze-colored 28-gauge craft wire
- .018" (.46mm) bronze-finish flexible beading wire
- 1 bronze-colored 2" (5cm) flat link curb chain
- 2 copper 2 x 2mm crimps
- 2 copper 4mm wire guardians
- 1 copper 6mm jump ring
- 2 copper 4mm jump rings
- 1 copper lobster claw clasp

**TOOLKIT**
- Diagonal wire cutters
- Round-nosed pliers
- Flat-nosed pliers (2 pairs)
- Two-step crimping pliers
- Bead stopper or paper clip

STAGE 1

See it **GROW**

**STAGE 1** Make four French beaded leaf dangles with four rows on each side (see Technique). Cut 16" (40cm) of craft wire and make another leaf with an extra row on each side. Cut 12" (30cm) of craft wire and make a final, smaller, leaf with just three rows on each side (not shown in this photograph; see Stage 5).

**STAGE 2** Cut 18" (46cm) of beading wire. String the largest French beaded dangle to the center. String [one jasper round, three chocolate brown seed beads, one glass leaf bead, three chocolate brown seed beads, one jasper round, and one medium French beaded dangle] twice on each side.

STAGE 2

STAGE 3

**STAGE 3** String [one jasper round, three chocolate brown seed beads, one glass leaf bead, and three chocolate brown seed beads] eight times on each side. Put a bead stopper or paper clip on one end of the wire.

## TECHNIQUE: FRENCH BEADED LEAF DANGLES

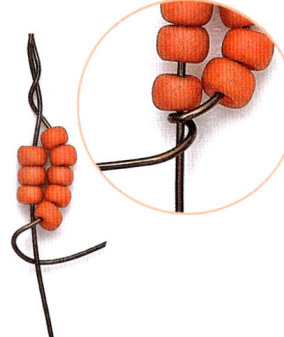   

**STEP 1**
Cut 14" (35cm) of craft wire. Fold over 4" (10cm) and make a twist about 1" (2.5cm) from the doubled end. String 3 seed beads of one color on the short end and 5 seed beads of the same color on the long end.

**STEP 2**
Cross the long end over the short end, from right to left, below the 3 beads.

**STEP 3**
Wrap the long end round under the short end, from left to right, then take it over the short end again from right to left (inset) to make a complete loop around the vertical wire.

**STEP 4**
String 7 beads of a different color onto the long end. Hold these beads close to the previous row and wrap the long end around the doubled wire above the beads. Make sure you always take the long end over, then under, then over again, so loops are on the back of the piece.

**STEP 5**
String another row of beads and wrap the long end around the short end below the beads. Add 3–4 more beads to each subsequent row, so that there are no gaps.

**STEP 6**
Repeat until there are four rows of the second color, two on each side. Add one more row of a third color on each side.

**STAGE 4** At the other end, string a jasper round, a crimp tube, another jasper round, and a wire guardian. Pass the wire carefully through the other end of the wire guardian and back through the first few beads. Secure the crimp with crimping pliers (see page 22). Take off the bead stopper and repeat the crimping steps at the other end, adjusting tension so no bare wire shows. Trim the spare ends of wire.

**STAGE 5** Use the 6mm jump ring and pliers (see page 23) to attach the smallest French beaded leaf to one end of the piece of chain.

**STAGE 6** Attach the other end of the chain to one end of the necklace with a 4mm jump ring. Use the last jump ring to attach the lobster claw clasp to the other end.

**Finished necklace:** Adjustable between 16 and 18" (40 and 45cm)

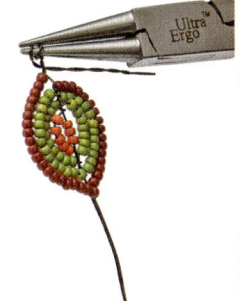
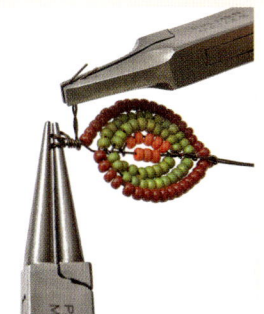

**STEP 7**
Hold both wires together at the base of the leaf and twist them together with pliers. Now use this twisted wire to make a double wrapped loop with round-nosed pliers (see page 24). Wrap the wire twice around the jaws of the pliers.

**STEP 8**
Use flat-nosed pliers to wrap the free end of the twisted wire securely around the wire below the double loop. Trim the ends short and neaten the coil with the round notch of the two-step crimping pliers (see page 22).

**STEP 9**
Squeeze the doubled wire at the tip of the leaf tightly together with the flat-nosed pliers.

**STEP 10**
Thread on one more seed bead in the third color. Turn a tiny loop in the end with round-nosed pliers.

**STEP 11**
Use flat-nosed pliers to coil the loop into a flat spiral. Vary the colors and pattern of the beads you use to make the other leaves, but keep the outermost rows chocolate brown.

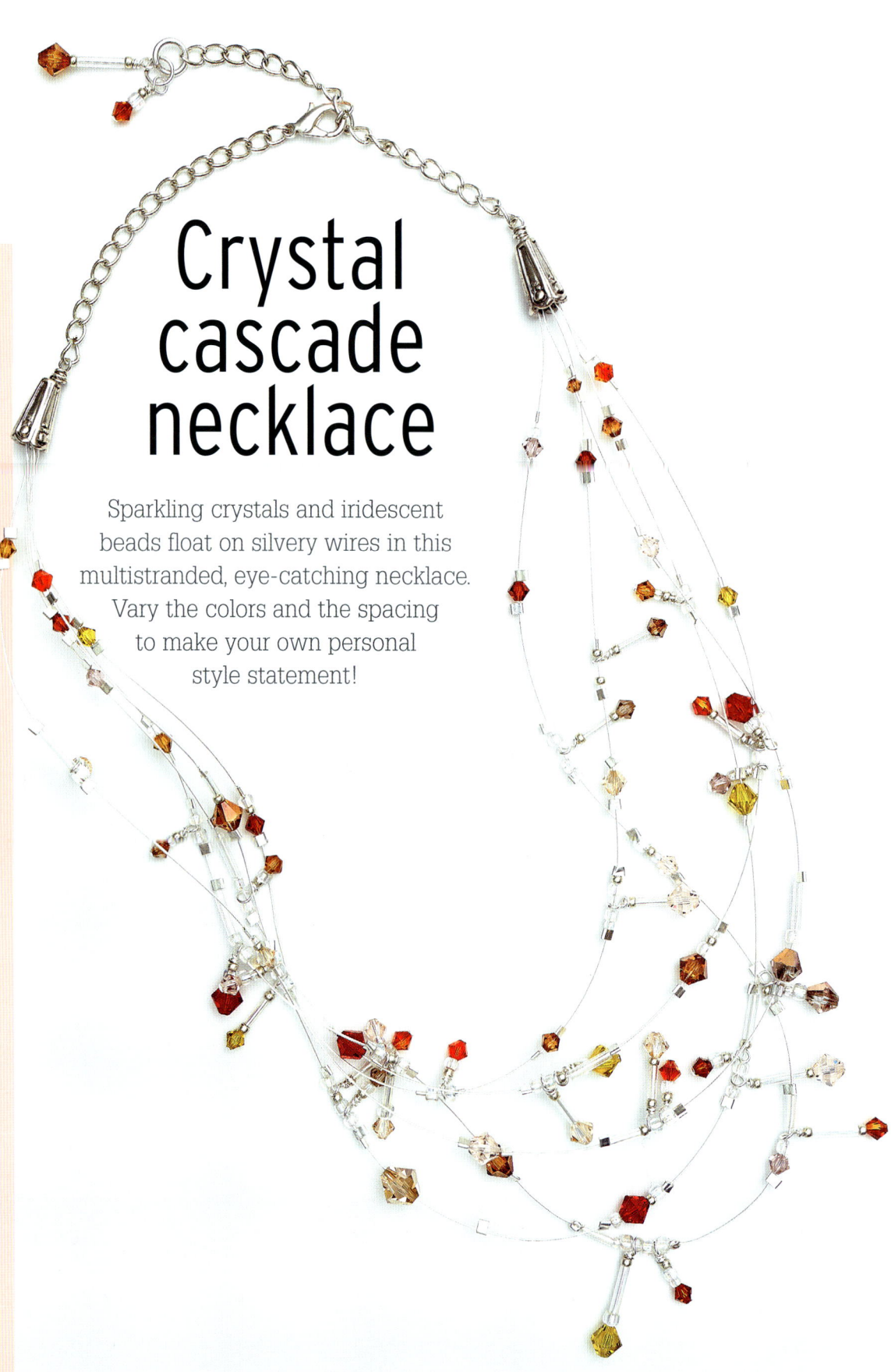

# Crystal cascade necklace

Sparkling crystals and iridescent beads float on silvery wires in this multistranded, eye-catching necklace. Vary the colors and the spacing to make your own personal style statement!

## YOU WILL NEED

### BEAD BOX

- 50 (approx.) 11º seed beads in two colors, silver-colored and transparent rainbow
- 20-25 transparent rainbow 8º seed beads
- 10 transparent rainbow 8º triangles
- 25 (approx.) transparent rainbow 6mm and/or 10mm bugle beads
- 70-80 crystal bicones in eight to ten colors and a mix of sizes between 4 and 8mm

### HARDWARE

- 25 (approx.) silver 1" (25mm) headpins
- .018" (.46mm) bright silver-finish flexible beading wire
- 90-100 (approx.) silver 2 x 2mm crimp tubes
- 2 silver 2" (50mm) eyepins
- 2 silver 1" (25mm) end cones
- 6-8" (15-20cm) silver medium curb chain
- Silver clasp of your choice
- 1 silver 6mm jump ring
- 1 silver 4mm jump ring

### TOOLKIT

- Round-nosed pliers
- Flat-nosed pliers (two pairs)
- Two-step crimping pliers
- Diagonal wire cutters

**Finished necklace:**
Approximately 16" (40cm) long

**See it GROW**

**STAGE 1** Use 1" (25mm) headpins to make approximately 25 wrapped-loop dangles with different combinations of crystals and beads, adding a silver 11º bead as the final bead on each one (see page 24). Set two dangles aside and divide the rest into five roughly equal groups. Divide the remaining crystal beads between these five groups too.

**STAGE 2** Cut five lengths of beading wire, starting with a piece 15" (38cm) long and increasing the length of each piece by 1" (2.5cm). The longest piece should be 19" (48cm) long. String a crimp tube on each piece in turn, and pass the end of the wire back through the tube, leaving a small loop. Secure with crimping pliers (see page 22) and trim the end very short.

**STAGE 3** Start with the shortest strand. String approximately eight single crystals or small clusters of beads and dangles, making sure there is a crimp before and after every cluster. Space the clusters out along the wire.

**STAGE 4** Squash the crimps to hold the clusters in place. Note that crimping pliers are not used in this stage, because there is only a single thickness of wire passing through the crimp. Flatten the crimp completely with flat-nosed pliers.

**STAGE 5** Repeat Stages 3–4 with the other strands, using gradually more clusters as the strands get longer. The final strand will have about 13 groups, each crimped on either side. Finish each strand with a crimp tube, as in Stage 2.

**STAGE 6** Use pliers to twist open the loop of an eyepin (see page 23). Hook it through the loop at one end of each strand. Close the eyepin loop. Repeat with the other eyepin at the other end of the strands.

**STAGE 7** Thread an end cone onto the first eyepin, wide end first. Slide it down so that it hides the ends of the wires. Make a wrapped loop above the end cone. Repeat with the second end cone at the other end.

STAGE 1

STAGES 3–5

**STAGE 4 (detail)**

Squash the crimps to hold each of the beads and clusters in place.

**STAGE 8** Cut the chain in half and attach one half to the wrapped loop above each end cone. Attach one half of the clasp to one free end of the chain; attach the 6mm jump ring to the other free end. Use the remaining jump ring to attach the two reserved dangles to the loop end.

STAGE 6

STAGE 7

# Oval pendant

Combine seed beads, accents, and metal components to create a multistranded, textural necklace that displays a gorgeous, handmade lampwork focal bead to full advantage.

## YOU WILL NEED

### BEAD BOX
- 22 topaz AB 8º Japanese seed beads
- 2g (approx.) 11º Japanese seed beads in each of three colors: terracotta, topaz AB, and matte silver-lined chartreuse
- 30 assorted glass, metal, and wooden accent beads ranging from 4mm to 10mm—try to have at least 8 pairs that match
- 3 olive and white 14 x 7mm handmade lampwork glass saucer beads
- 10 copper 11º metal seed beads
- 5 brown 3mm crystal bicones
- 1 rust, white, and olive 40 x 25mm handmade lampwork glass oval tab focal bead

### HARDWARE
- .018" (.46mm) flexible beading wire
- 10 silver 2 x 2mm crimp tubes
- 12 copper 4mm jump rings
- 2 copper 3-to-1 connector links
- 1 copper 10mm lobster claw clasp
- 1 copper 6mm jump ring
- 8 copper 2" (50mm) headpins
- 5" (12.5cm) copper 22-gauge craft wire
- 1 copper 8mm jump ring

### TOOLKIT
- Diagonal wire cutters
- Round-nosed pliers
- Flat-nosed pliers (2 pairs)
- Magical crimping pliers

**Finished pendant:**
Approximately 17" (43cm) long

**See it GROW**

**STAGE 1** Cut three 10" (25cm) lengths of beading wire. On each one, string a crimp tube and a 8º seed bead. Pass the end back through the bead and crimp, leaving a small loop. Secure the crimp with crimping pliers (see page 42). String two 8º seed beads and then start stringing 11º seed beads onto the free end of the wire, making sure the short end goes through the first few beads (trim if necessary).

**STAGE 1**

**STAGE 2** When the seed-bead strand is approximately 7½" (19cm) long, string two 8º seed beads, a crimp, and another 8º seed bead. Put the end of the wire back through the last few beads, pull to form a small loop, secure the crimp, and trim the wire end. Repeat to make three similar strands, one of each color.

**STAGE 3** Use 4mm jump rings to attach one hole of a 3-to-1 connector link to each end of each seed-bead strand (see page 23).

**STAGE 4** Cut two 7" (18cm) lengths of wire. Add a crimp and a 8º seed bead to one end of each and make a loop, as in Stage 1. String a graduated sequence of accent beads plus a lampwork saucer, separating them with 11º seed beads. Finish with another crimp and a 8º seed bead and make another loop.

**STAGE 5** Attach the end with the larger beads to the single hole end of the 3-to-1 connector link holding the seed-bead strands. Repeat to make a matching second strand for the other side of the necklace.

**STAGE 6** Use a 4mm jump ring to attach the clasp to one end of the necklace. Make a wrapped-loop dangle with the third lampwork saucer, a couple of small accent beads and a metal seed bead. (see page 24). Attach this dangle and the 6mm jump ring to the other end of the necklace.

STAGE 2

STAGE 3

STAGE 4

STAGE 5

STAGE 6

## PENDANT ASSEMBLY

**STAGE 7**
Use the remaining accent beads, bicones, and seed beads to make seven small wrapped-loop dangles, with a copper metal seed bead at the top of each one. Attach dangles to 4mm jump rings in the configurations shown.

**STAGE 8**
Connect the rings together to form a tassel.

**STAGE 9**
Make a wrapped loop at one end of the length of craft wire. String a metal seed bead, 3mm crystal bicone, the focal bead, another 3mm bicone, and a metal seed bead.

**STAGE 10**
Make another wrapped loop at the other end of the wire. Attach this loop to the 8mm jump ring. Attach the top ring of the dangle tassel to the other end of the focal pendant. Open the jump ring on the pendant and close it over all three seed-bead strands.

Make a wire-wrapped loop.

**See it GROW**

**STAGE 1** String a leaf bead and a silver round onto an eyepin and make a wire-wrapped loop at the top (see page 24). The loop you make should be on the same plane as the loop at the bottom of the eyepin (see Orientation of dangles, opposite).

**STAGE 2** Use flat-nosed pliers and a 4mm jump ring (see page 23) to attach the top loop of a 2-to-1 connector link to the bottom of the eyepin.

**STAGE 3** Make two more eyepin dangles in the same way, except that this time the wrapped loop should be at 90 degrees to the loop at the bottom.

**STAGE 4** Use flat-nosed pliers and 3mm jump rings to attach one leaf dangle to each of the bottom loops of the 2-to-1 link.

## YOU WILL NEED

**BEAD BOX**
- 6 light moss green 11 x 8mm glass birch leaves
- 18 silver 2mm round beads
- 12 smoked topaz 2mm crystal bicones
- 8 copper crystal 3mm crystal bicones
- 4 lime 3mm crystal bicones
- 4 lime 4mm crystal bicones
- 4 olivine 4mm crystal bicones
- 4 topaz 4mm crystal bicones
- 12 topaz and/or chartreuse 11° seed beads

**HARDWARE**
- 6 silver 1" (25mm) eyepins
- 2 silver 4mm jump rings
- 2 pewter or silver 2-to-1 connector links
- 6 silver 3mm jump rings
- 12 silver fine-gauge 1" (25mm) headpins
- 1 pair silver earwires

**TOOLKIT**
- Round-nosed pliers
- Flat-nosed pliers (2 pairs)
- Diagonal wire cutters

# Spring birch earrings

Cascading chandelier earrings are simple to make. In this project you will use 2-to-1 connectors and your own wire-wrapped eyepin links to create delicate dangles of glass leaves and crystals with lots of sparkle and movement, recalling the first leaves on the birch trees waving in a spring breeze.

**Tip Chandelier options** There are many pretty chandelier findings on the market, so have fun finding your favorites and adorning them with dangles and links. If you prefer shorter earrings, omit the first leaf and attach the 2-to-1 link directly to the earwire.

Add dangles below the leaves.

These earrings seem simple but they are designed with great care to ensure that everything hangs as it should. Notice how the crystal clusters are arranged so that they are mirror images of each other: it's the little details like this that really make a design look professional.

**STAGE 5** String crystals, seed beads, and silver rounds onto each of three headpins, as shown in the photograph, making three dangles of different lengths. String a second, identical set of three dangles. Make wire-wrapped loops at the top of each dangle.

**STAGE 6** Open a 3mm jump ring and string three dangles on it in the sequence: shortest, longest, medium. Attach to the bottom of one of the eyepins, with the shortest dangle toward the center of the earring.

**STAGE 7** Do the same with the other set of three dangles, again with the shortest toward the center. Attach an earwire to the top of the top eyepin. Make another earring in the same way.

## ORIENTATION OF DANGLES

The geometry of your findings is very important when you're making designs with linked dangles, particularly earrings. Pay close attention to the orientation of the loops on your earwires and connectors in order to make sure everything hangs the right way round. In the style shown here, for example, all three loops on the connectors are on the same plane, but sometimes one or more of the loops is at 90 degrees, so the wire-wrapped loops on your eyepin dangles may need to be at 90 degrees too, otherwise the crystals at the bottom will be hanging sideways.

**Finished earrings:**
Approximately 3" (7.5cm) long

Twist gently until the loops are in the correct position.

It's not always possible to create a wire-wrapped loop in exactly the direction you intended, and you may find you have wrongly predicted how everything will hang. To change the orientation of loops at the top and bottom of an eyepin link, hold each loop in a pair of pliers, one in each hand, and twist gently until the loops are in the correct position. Before you start to twist, check that the pliers are gripping only the wire, to avoid squashing or breaking any beads.

## YOU WILL NEED

**BEAD BOX**
- 120 (approx.) mixed green and purple 4-8mm accent beads, including firepolished rounds, silver tubes, pewter Bali spacers, and pressed glass hearts (A)
- 2 silver 8mm flower spacers (B)
- 10 silver 4mm flower spacers (C)
- 2 green and purple 30mm lampwork glass heart focals (D)
- 30 (approx.) silver 2mm rounds (E)
- 7 matte green 12mm pressed glass ovals (F)
- 5g (approx.) matte and/or transparent purple 8° seed beads (G)

**HARDWARE**
- .018" (.46mm) flexible beading wire
- 4 silver 2 x 2mm crimp tubes
- 2 silver 4mm wire guardians
- 1 silver 6mm jump ring

**TOOLKIT**
- Diagonal wire cutters
- Bead stoppers or paper clips
- Flat-nosed pliers (2 pairs)
- Magical crimping pliers

**Finished lariat** Approximately 42" (106cm) long

# Lilac lariat

Pretty pale greens and purples bring a breath of summertime to this long, sinuous lariat necklace. The design features a non-matching pair of handmade heart focals complemented with a mixture of glass and silver beads. Pick your own selection of treasures from your bead box, and create your own combination!

**See it GROW**

**STAGE 1** Cut 24" (60cm) of beading wire and put a bead stopper or paper clip on one end. String a crimp tube followed by A, B, A, C, A, D, A, C, and E. Pull about 2½" (6.5cm) of wire through the beads.

**STAGE 2** Bring the short end of the wire back through all the beads except the final E, and through the crimp. Use crimping pliers to secure the crimp (see page 42). Trim the short end of wire close to the crimp.

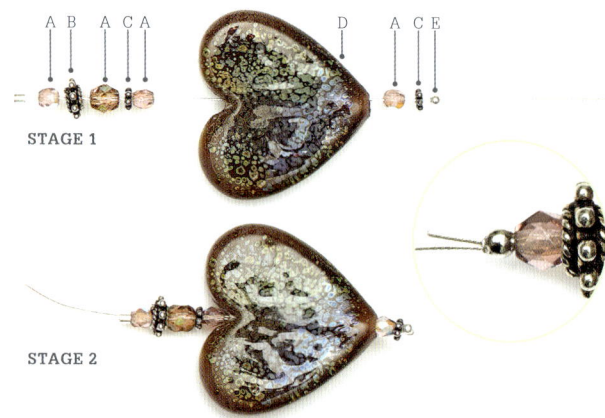

A B  A C A    D   A C E

**STAGE 1**

**STAGE 2**

**STAGE 3**

**STAGE 3** Set aside 4 A beads that match the ones just strung, for the other end of the lariat. Divide the remaining A beads into six roughly equal groups.

**STAGE 4** String an F bead, making sure it goes over the short end of wire to hide it. Now string one of your groups of A beads, using E and G beads in between the larger As, to give more flexibility. End with an E bead.

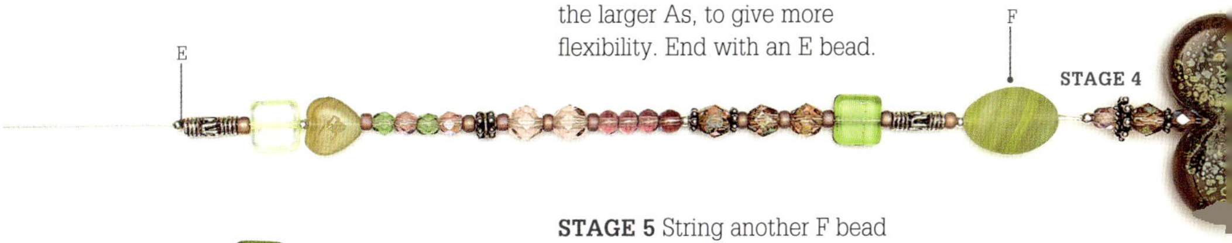

E

F

**STAGE 4**

**STAGE 5** String another F bead followed by a group of A beads with Es and Gs in between as in Stage 4. Do this one more time for a total of three sections.

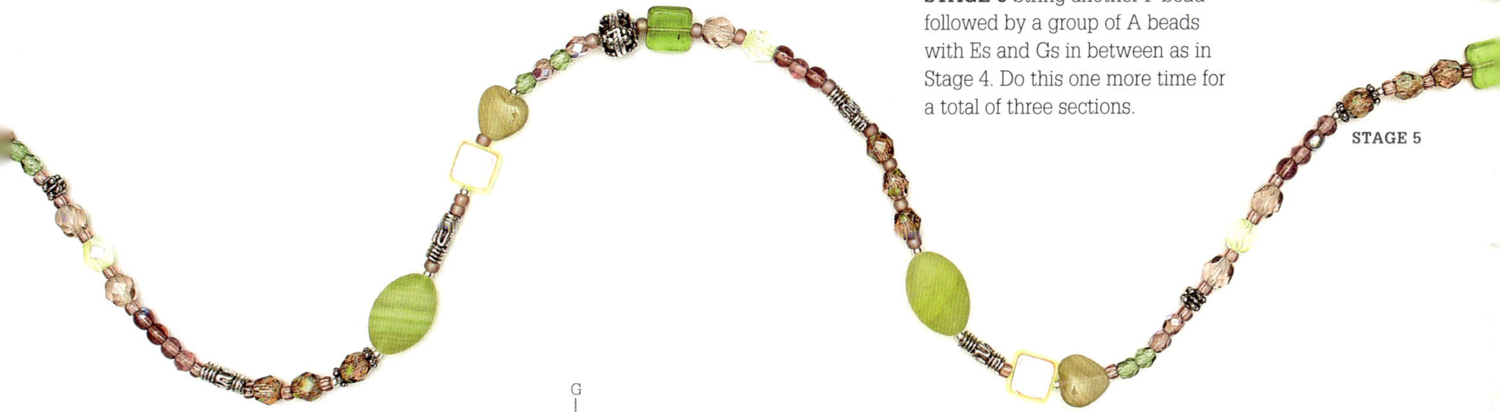

**STAGE 5**

G

**STAGE 6**

**STAGE 7**

**STAGE 6** End the section with a crimp tube, a G bead, and a wire guardian. Go back through the G bead, the crimp, and a few more beads, making sure there is no bare wire but not pulling too tight. Secure the crimp and trim the short end of wire.

**STAGE 7** Make the other half of the lariat in the same way, working through Stages 1–6. End the section this time with your final F bead.

**STAGE 8**

**STAGE 8** Open the jump ring (see page 23) and use it to connect the two wire guardians together. This gives a safety breakpoint in the center of the lariat.

Use a jump ring to create a safety breakpoint.

## LARIAT STYLE

Some ideas for tying your new lariat:

**1 Single loop** Just wrap one end around the other

**2 Overhand knot** Tie a knot with both strands together

**3 Slip knot** Fold in two and put the ends through the loop

**4 Wraparound** Try it with the ends at the back

**5 Wraparound with single loop** Combine two knots for extra interest

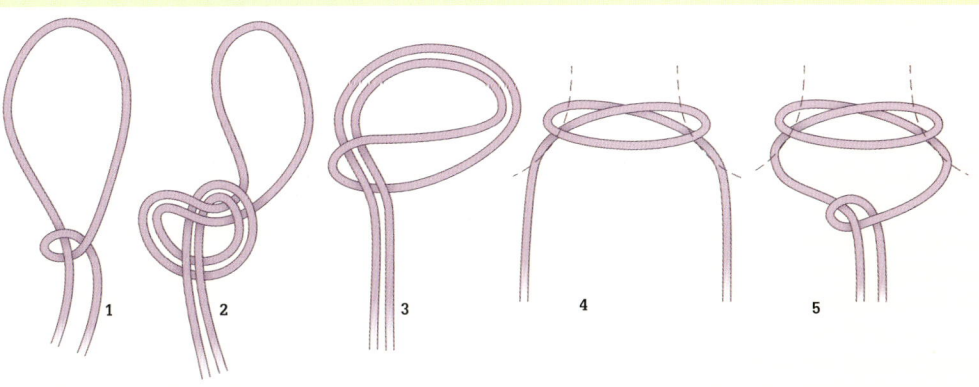

1    2    3    4    5

# Forest glade necklace

This elegant necklace with malachite and copper evokes flecks of sunlight glinting through lush green leaves. Simple stringing plus a little bit of bead stitching makes a luxuriant tassel to complement an art glass focal bead.

**Finished necklace:** Approximately 20" (50cm) long

## TECHNIQUE: STITCHING A TASSEL

**STEP 1**
Thread your needle with about 4' (1.2m) of thread and tie on a single A to act as a stop bead; if possible, use a contrast color that makes it clear to see.

**STEP 2**
Stitch through two A beads of the foundation loop on your necklace.

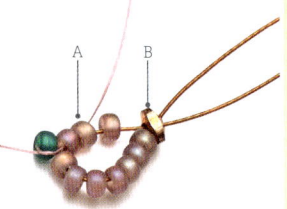

**STEP 3**
Pull the thread gently through the beads until the stop bead rests against the loop.

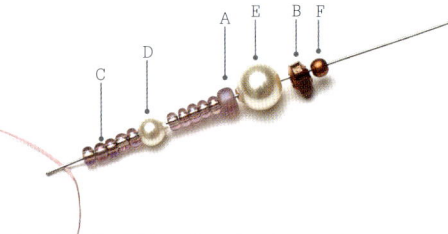

**STEP 4**
Start a fringe. Pick up five Cs, one D, five Cs, and one each of A, E, B, and F.

## YOU WILL NEED

### BEAD BOX

- 30 (approx.) matte transparent emerald 8º seed beads (A)
- 40 (approx.) copper 4mm glass washers (B)
- 2g (approx.) matte transparent emerald 11º seed beads (C)
- 17 cream 3mm round glass pearls (D)
- 19 cream 4mm round glass pearls (E)
- 55 copper 2mm round beads (F)
- 5 matte emerald vitrail 12 x 7mm glass leaves (G)
- 42 malachite 6mm round beads (H)
- 12 copper 4mm flower spacers (I)
- 8 copper 6 x 5mm hollow leaf charms (J)
- 1 green and cream 15mm round handmade lampwork focal

### HARDWARE

- .018" (.46mm) satin copper finish flexible beading wire
- Dark green K.O. nylon beading thread
- 2 copper 2 x 2mm crimp tubes
- 2 copper 4mm wire guardians
- 1 copper 20mm floral S-hook clasp (or clasp of your choice)
- 2 copper 4mm jump rings
- 2 copper 6mm jump rings

### TOOLKIT

- Diagonal wire cutters
- Bead stoppers or paper clips
- Beading needle
- Flat-nosed pliers (2 pairs)
- Two-step crimping pliers

**See it GROW**

**STAGE 1** Cut approximately 24" (60cm) of beading wire. String 10 As to serve as the foundation loop for the tassel. Slide them to the center of the wire. String a B over both ends of the wire. Slide it down to the beads and put a bead stopper or paper clip on both wire ends to keep the loop in shape.

**STAGE 2** Stitch the tassel (see Technique). Note: This can be done at the end of the project if you prefer, but if bead stitching is new to you, you will find it easier to do it without the rest of the necklace to get in your way!

**STAGE 3** Take off the bead stopper or paper clip. On both ends of the wire, string a B, the lampwork focal, and another B. Slide them right down to the tassel.

**Tip** **Focal choice** This adaptable basic construction is a great way of showcasing a beautiful handmade bead. Just remember that if you have a round focal and it's bigger than 15mm, it will stick out from the wearer's neck. Flattened lampwork shapes such as lentils or tabs avoid this problem. They are also lighter in weight for a bigger visible area.

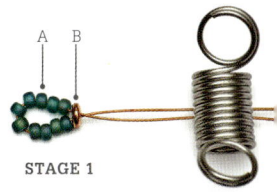

STAGE 1

STAGE 2

STAGE 3

Continued next page

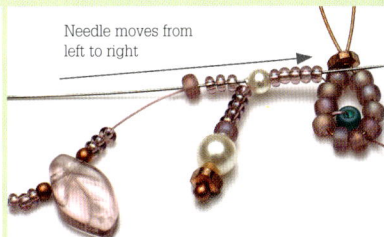

### STEP 5
Skip the last bead (the F) and stitch carefully back through the remaining beads, bringing your needle out of the one before the D.

### STEP 6
Pull the thread through the beads until no bare thread is showing.

### STEP 7
Make a branch. Pick up three Cs, one A, three Cs, one each of F, G, and F, and three Cs.

### STEP 8
Stitch back through the 8º and all remaining beads of the fringe, and pull the thread so that the leaf and the beads either side of it form a loop. Don't pull too tight or your fringe will be too rigid to hang elegantly.

STAGE 4

C A F B E B F H I H

**STAGE 4** On one wire, string one C and an A. Then string [F, B, E, B, F, H, I, H, I, H].

**STAGE 5** Repeat the bracketed stringing sequence five times, replacing the spacers between the malachite beads with C and D in subsequent repeats. End with a single H bead.

**STAGE 6** Repeat the stringing sequence on the other strand.

C                D

STAGE 5

STAGE 7

**STAGE 7** Finish each end with a crimp tube, a washer, and a wire guardian. Pass the wire around the guardian loop and back through the washer, the crimp, and the final bead. Secure the crimps with crimping pliers (see page 22) and trim the wire ends.

## TECHNIQUE: STITCHING A TASSEL CONTINUED

**STEP 9**
Stitch through the next bead of the foundation loop and stitch another branched fringe. Make each successive fringe longer by adding an extra C after the D, and on alternate fringes replace the E and B with H and I, and replace the leaf (G) with a pair of charms (J).

**STEP 10**
Keep making the fringes longer until you have a total of five fringes. You are now at the center of your tassel.

**STEP 11**
Stitch a further four fringes, making them shorter so that the second half of the tassel mirrors the first. You should have a total of nine fringes for this project.

**STEP 12**
After finishing the last fringe, stitch back through all the beads of the foundation loop.

**STAGE 8**

**STAGE 8** Attach the clasp to two 6mm jump rings (see page 23). Close one side of the "S" and make sure the other is open enough to allow the ring to detach. Use 4mm jump rings to attach the 6mm rings to each end of the necklace.

## OTHER TASSELS

If the idea of bead stitching doesn't appeal to you, there are other methods of adding a tassel. An easy way is to take short lengths of silk thread, add a couple of beads, tie a double knot at each end, fold in half, and attach to the bottom loop with a lark's-head knot (see page 39). Or create a tassel with chain (see Summer Nights Earrings, page 46), or build your own chain from jump rings (see page 78). Experiment until you find a look that works for you!

**STEP 13**
Your thread should exit the foundation loop in the same place as your tail thread with the stop bead on it.

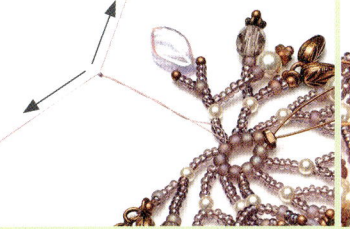

**STEP 14**
Untie the stop bead. Align the threads so they are parallel, and tie a single overhand knot in both threads together. Pull the ends apart slowly and firmly in opposite directions, so the knot travels right down to the loop and is hidden. (This technique will only work with K.O. thread. With other types of nylon beading thread you will have to weave in the ends and knot them separately.)

**STEP 15**
Weave both thread ends through to the end of a fringe, and trim the spare thread.

## YOU WILL NEED

### BEAD BOX

- 1 red and green 20 x 10mm lampwork glass bird bead
- 20 bronze 4mm glass flower spacers (A)
- 54 cranberry gold luster 8º seed beads (B)
- 18 red and green 10mm glass pears (C)
- 9 olive vitrail 12 x 7mm glass leaves (D)
- 9 emerald matte vitrail 12 x 7mm glass leaves (E)
- 18 Siam gold luster 6mm cathedral beads (F)
- 18 brass 11º seed beads (G)

### HARDWARE

- .018" (.46mm) satin copper-finish flexible beading wire
- 6 copper 2 x 2mm crimp tubes
- 6 brass 4mm jump rings
- 1 oxidized brass 3-strand sliding clasp

### TOOLKIT

- Diagonal wire cutters
- Bead stoppers or paper clips
- Flat-nosed pliers (2 pairs)
- Two-step crimping pliers

**Finished bracelet:**
Approximately 7" (18cm) long

# Pear tree bracelet

A partridge in a pear tree—just the thing for a festive holiday gift. This colorful, tactile bracelet, with its little glass bird perched amid a garland of fruits and leaves, will become a favorite all year round.

STAGE 1

STAGE 2

**See it GROW**

**STAGE 1** Cut three 10" (25cm) lengths of wire and put the ends into a bead stopper or paper clips. On all three wires, string an A bead, the focal bird bead, then another A, and slide to the center.

**STAGE 2** Now work with one wire at a time. String a B, then [C, B, D, B, F, A, G] three times, substituting an E for the D in the second repeat. Put a bead stopper on the end of the wire.

**STAGE 3** On the second strand, string [B, E, B, F, A, G, C] three times, substituting a D for the E in the second repeat.

**STAGE 4** On the third strand, string [B, F, A, G, C, B, D] three times, substituting an E for the D in the second repeat.

STAGE 3

STAGE 4

STAGE 5

STAGE 6

**STAGE 5** String the other side of the bracelet in exactly the same way, starting the sequence in a different place on each strand.

**STAGE 6** Finish each end in turn with an A bead, a crimp tube, and another A. Pass the wire back through the last few beads, leaving a small loop. Secure the crimps (see page 22) and trim the wire ends. Make sure there is as little bare wire as possible before you crimp the other end of the bracelet.

**STAGE 7** Attach each end in turn to one loop of the clasp, using the jump rings (see page 23).

**STAGE 8** Use the remaining jump rings to attach the other end of the bracelet to the other side of the clasp.

STAGE 7

STAGE 8

These earrings are ideal for experimentation. Substitute 8º seed beads for the triangle beads if you like, or try using red in place of the big green beads. You can add more dangles, or mix up the beads for a more disorganized look.

**Finished earrings:** Approximately 2¹⁄₂" (6.5cm) excluding earwire

# Cherry harvest earrings

Making your own chain with jump rings is a fun and easy way to add length and movement to a pair of earrings.

## YOU WILL NEED

### BEAD BOX

- 2 transparent olive 12mm firepolished glass faceted rounds
- 2 transparent red AB 4mm glass rounds
- 6 transparent olive 10mm glass leaves, drilled lengthwise
- 2 transparent red 6mm glass rounds
- 22 dark red Picasso 4mm firepolished rounds
- 20 (approx.) silver-lined amethyst 11º seed beads
- 20 (approx.) copper-lined chartreuse 8º triangle beads
- 28 copper 2mm rounds

### HARDWARE

- Pair of copper 2" (5cm) eyepins
- 30 copper 1" (2.5cm) fine-gauge headpins
- 2 copper 6mm jump rings
- Pair of copper earwires
- 10 copper 4mm jump rings

### TOOLKIT

- Flat-nosed pliers (two pairs)
- Round-nosed pliers
- One-step looper (optional)
- Diagonal wire cutters

**Tip Make your own chain** Maybe you need an extender chain at the back of a necklace? Is a bracelet you made just a half-inch too tight? Connect up some jump rings (see Technique), and the problem's solved.

## TECHNIQUE: MAKING A CHAIN

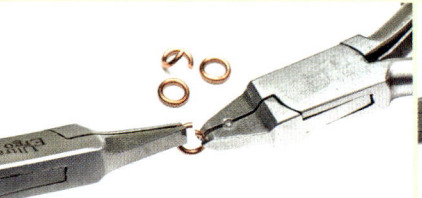

**STEP 1**
Use two pairs of flat-nosed pliers to open half of your jump rings (see page 23) and make sure the rest are neatly closed.

**STEP 2**
Connect two closed rings with one open ring. Close the open ring.

**STEP 3**
Connect the second closed ring to a third, and so on until your chain is long enough.

**STEP 4**
For a more robust chain, simply double up the rings.

Wrap the wire in a haphazard style and don't trim the ends, just press them into the wire coil with the tips of your flat-nosed pliers.

**See it GROW**

Dangle 1   Dangle 2   Dangle 3

**STAGE 1** String an A, a B, and a C on an eyepin. Use a one-step looper or round-nosed pliers to make a loop at the top of the eyepin.

**STAGE 2** Create wrapped-loop dangles (see page 24) with headpins and beads as follows: Make ?? dangles (Dangle 1) with D, E or C, and F. Make six with G and F (Dangle 2) and a final two dangles with H and C (Dangle 3).

**STAGE 3** Open a 6mm jump ring and string on a pair of Dangle 1, the top loop of the eyepin from Stage 1, a Dangle 2, another Dangle 1, and the loop of an earwire. Close the jump ring.

**STAGE 4** Open a 4mm jump ring. Add a Dangle 3, a pair of Dangle 1, and the bottom loop of the eyepin from Stage 1. Close the jump ring.

**STAGE 5** Open another 4mm jump ring. Add a Dangle 2 and a Dangle 1. Close the jump ring around the jump ring you added in Stage 4, making sure you add the new jump ring in between the two dangles on the previous ring.

**STAGE 6** Open a third 4mm jump ring. Add a pair of Dangle 1 and connect to the ring you added in Stage 5, again making sure that the new ring is between the two dangles on the previous ring.

**STAGE 7** Repeat, adding a pair of Dangle 1 again.

**STAGE 8** Add a fifth and final 4mm jump ring with a Dangle 1 and a Dangle 2. Repeat all stages to make the second earring.

Lush clusters of wire-wrapped charms adorn the centerpiece of this rustic chain necklace with its double clasp. The colors are perfect for the holidays, and the design makes a versatile base for your own selection of favorite beads.

# Charm cluster necklace

Wrapped-loop dangles x 44

**See it GROW**

**STAGE 1** Use the accent beads, triangles, seed beads, spacers, and headpins to make 44 wrapped-loop dangles with rustic loops (see page 24). Divide the dangles into 11 groups of four.

**STAGE 2** Connect each group into a cluster with a 6mm jump ring (see page 23).

**STAGE 3** Add a second 6mm jump ring to the top of each cluster.

**STAGE 4** Connect two clusters together with a third 6mm jump ring.

## YOU WILL NEED

### BEAD BOX
- 44 assorted red and olive green 6-12mm accent beads, including ceramic hearts, firepolished glass rounds, glass leaves, and cathedral beads
- 12-14 bronze, red, white and/or purple 4mm glass flower spacers
- 44 copper-lined chartreuse 8º Japanese triangle beads
- 44 copper 11º metal seed beads

### HARDWARE
- 44 copper 2" (50mm) headpins
- 33 copper 6mm jump rings
- 2 copper 2 x 4mm ribbon end crimps
- 9" (23cm) (approx.) olive green 4mm faux suede lace
- 2 copper 4mm jump rings
- 2 copper 16mm toggle clasps

### TOOLKIT
- Diagonal wire cutters
- Round-nosed pliers
- Flat-nosed pliers (2 pairs)

**Finished necklace:** Approximately 18" (45cm) long

**STAGE 5** Connect a third cluster to the second one with a jump ring, and continue in the same way until all the clusters are connected, forming a chain with clusters on alternate loops.

STAGE 5

## TECHNIQUE: BRACELET CONVERSION AND MATCHING EARRINGS

**STEP 1**
To wear the central section as a bracelet, you will need the toggle parts of two more clasps. Connect them together with jump rings as shown. Add a charm to the central connecting rings if you like.

**STEP 2**
Undo the clasps on the necklace and use the double toggle to fasten the chain section into a bracelet.

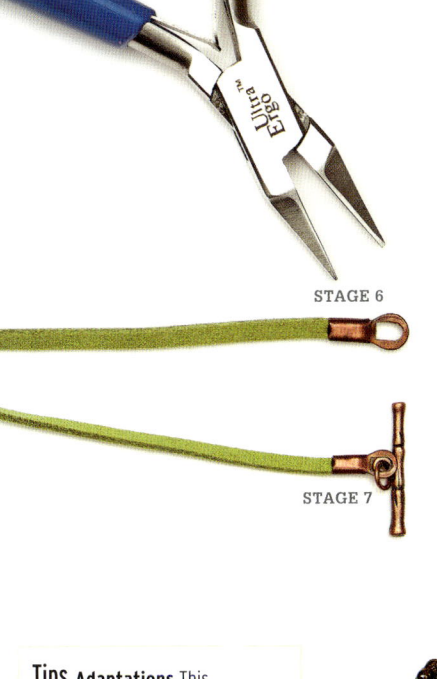

**STAGE 6** Attach a ribbon end crimp (see page 33) to each end of the suede lace.

**STAGE 7** Use the 4mm jump rings to attach the toggle parts of the clasps to the end crimps. Attach the clasp rings to the first and last 6mm jump rings of the chain section.

STAGE 6

STAGE 7

STAGE 7

STAGE 8

**STAGE 8** Fasten both toggles to complete the necklace.

**Tips Adaptations** This construction lends itself to all sorts of modifications. Change copper to silver, suede to silk ribbon, and accent beads to crystals, for a stunning party piece. You could add a focal bead in the center, or make several graduated strands at the front.

**Complete the package** You can convert the center section of your necklace to a bracelet, and add a pair of matching earrings (see Technique).

**STEP 3**
Now use the ring parts of the extra clasps to make earrings. Connect an earwire to the loop of each ring.

**STEP 4**
Make six clusters of four charms, following Stages 1–2 of the necklace.

**STEP 5**
Connect three clusters together, so you have a row of three jump rings. Repeat with the remaining three clusters.

**STEP 6**
Use an extra jump ring to connect each set of the three clusters to the bottom of an earwire.

# Misty mountains collar

Who said gray was boring? Learn how to handle a multistranded stringing project as you construct this head-turning, sophisticated collar with its subtly scalloped shape and monochrome palette. Pearls, silver, seed beads, glass, and labradorite all play their part in adding detail and sparkle. Spacer bars keep everything together and allow the full beauty of all the beads to be seen.

## YOU WILL NEED

### BEAD BOX

- 80 labradorite 4mm rounds (A)
- 5g gunmetal 8º seed beads (B)
- 15 clear AB 4mm firepolished glass rounds (C)
- 100 labradorite 6 x 2mm center-drilled disks (D)
- 25 gray 8mm freshwater pearls (E)
- 62 stone gray luster 4mm firepolished glass rounds (F)
- 10 vitrail half-coated 6mm firepolished glass rounds (G)
- 5 silver 8 x 7mm Bali ball spacers (H)

### HARDWARE

- .018" (.46mm) flexible beading wire
- 6 silver 23 x 8mm 5-hole spacer bars
- 10 silver 2 x 2mm crimp tubes
- 2 silver 2" (50mm) eyepins
- 4 silver 4mm jump rings
- 2 silver 20 x 12mm Bali end cones
- 1 silver 20mm S-hook clasp with 2 rings (or clasp of your choice)

### TOOLKIT

- Diagonal wire cutters
- Bead stoppers or paper clips
- Flat-nosed pliers (2 pairs)
- Round-nosed pliers
- Two-step crimping pliers

**Finished collar:** Approximately 15" (38cm) long by 1½" (3.8cm) deep at center front

**STAGE 1**

A B C D E

**See it GROW**

**STAGE 1** Cut five pieces of wire 20" (50cm) long and put them all into a bead stopper or paper clip about 3" (7.5cm) from the end. String a spacer bar with one wire in each hole. Starting with what will be the shortest strand, string A, B, C, B, two Ds, E, two Ds, B, C, B, and A. Put a bead stopper or paper clip on each strand as you work downward.

**STAGE 2**

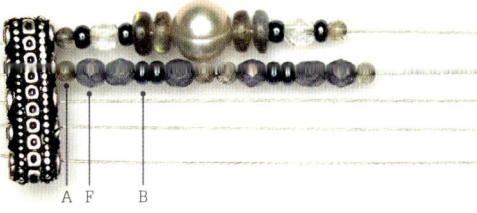

A F B

**STAGE 2** On the next strand down, string A, two Fs, two Bs, F, two As, F, two Bs, two Fs, and A.

**STAGE 3**

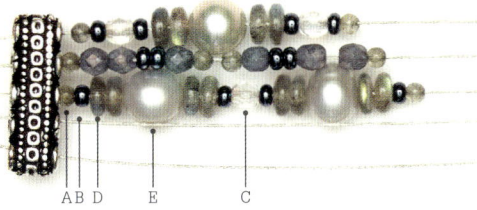

A B D E C

**STAGE 3** On the third wire, string A, B, two Ds, E, two Ds, B, C, B, two Ds, E, two Ds, B, and A.

**STAGE 4**

A F B G

**STAGE 4** On the fourth strand, string A, two Fs, two Bs, F, G, two Bs, G, F, two Bs, two Fs, and A.

**STAGE 5**

A B D E H

**STAGE 5** On the longest strand, string A, B, two Ds, E, two Ds, B, A, H, A, B, two Ds, E, two Ds, B, and A.

Continued next page

STAGE 5

**STAGE 6** Take off the bead stoppers or paper clips from the right-hand ends and string another spacer bar. Repeat the stringing sequences from Stages 1–5 to make four more sections, ending with a spacer bar.

STAGE 6

**Tip** **Test on the body** If the design doesn't seem to lie flat on your bead board, remember that it will be curved around your neck when you wear it. This will emphasize the length differences between the strands. Check in a mirror, or use a display bust if you have one, to see how the collar looks. You may need to adjust the bead counts (see Technique) if you're not happy with the curvature.

## TECHNIQUE: DIFFERENT WAYS TO CREATE A CURVE

**INCREASE THE SIZE**
Use progressively larger beads in each strand, starting with the smallest beads on the shortest strand. Adjust the bead counts until you have a smooth curve.

**INCREASE THE NUMBER**
Stick to the same size of bead and use a few more in each successive row to make your curve.

**MIX AND MATCH**
Adding more *and* larger beads to the longer strands will also create a curve. For a dramatic scalloped edge, increase the number and size of beads in the outer strand.

16B 17B 18B 19B 20B

STAGE 7

STAGE 8

F    B

STAGE 9

Don't pull the wire too tightly when you're crimping this piece together, just make sure there is no bare wire showing.

**STAGE 7** On the shortest strand, string 16 Bs. String 17 Bs, 18 Bs, 19 Bs, and 20 Bs on the next four strands, respectively. Put a crimp tube on the end of each strand. Take the wire back through the crimp and 4–5 more beads, then secure the crimp (see page 22) and trim the short end of wire. Repeat for all five strands.

**STAGE 8** Open a jump ring (see page 23) and use it to connect the ends of all the strands to the loop of an eyepin.

**STAGE 9** String an end cone onto the eyepin, followed by an F and a B. Make a wire-wrapped loop (see page 24). Now take the bead stopper off the other end of the collar, pull the wire carefully through all the beads and spacers, string beads as in Stage 7, and finish the other end in the same way.

**STAGE 10** Use the remaining two jump rings to connect the clasp to the collar.

STAGE 10

## TECHNIQUE: **STRAIGHT STRIP**

Simply keep all the strands the same length to create a wide flat strip for a bracelet or choker.

# Silk and stone bracelet

Learn to embrace imperfection in this adjustable boho-style bracelet with its mix of stone, glass, metal, and fabric. Rustic wire wrapping turns silk ribbon into links and tassels to soften the look.

## YOU WILL NEED

### BEAD BOX

- 24 copper 4mm washers or spacers
- 8 copper 6mm bicones
- 5 labradorite 10-12mm faceted nuggets
- 25-30 labradorite chips
- 3 labradorite 12mm coin beads
- 2 matte metallic coated 10mm Czech glass faceted rounds
- 8 matte metallic half-coated 4mm Czech glass peanut beads

### HARDWARE

- .018" (.46mm) satin copper-finish flexible beading wire
- 4 copper or silver 2 x 2mm crimp tubes
- 6" (15cm) of gray frayed sari silk ribbon
- 9" (23cm) of 22-gauge natural brass wire
- 2" (5cm) copper eyepin
- 7" (18cm) of 3.5 x 4mm natural brass small flat cable chain (the chain links must be open, not soldered—you should be able to open and close the links with pliers)
- 9 copper 4mm jump rings
- 9-10 links of 10mm natural brass round link chain (open or soldered)
- Brass hook clasp

### TOOLKIT

- Diagonal wire cutters
- Flat-nosed pliers
- Two-step crimping pliers
- Scissors
- Round-nosed pliers
- One-step looper (optional)

### STAGE 1

**Long strand** Cut a 10" (25cm) length of beading wire and string approximately 6" (15cm) of beads. Use the larger beads and all but one of the nuggets and coins: refer to the photograph, or invent your own sequence. Finish each end with a bicone, a crimp tube, and a washer.

**Short strand** Cut a 7" (18cm) length of cable and string approximately 4" (10cm) of beads, ending with a coin bead. (This strand will be joined to the ribbon section later.) String groups of smaller beads and chips with copper beads in between. Finish each end with a crimp tube and a washer.

**STAGE 2** On each strand in turn, take the end of the wire back through the last few beads, leaving a small loop of wire, and secure the crimp (see page 22). Push the beads together (not too tightly) and repeat the crimping at the other end.

Long strand

Short strand

**STAGE 1**

**STAGE 2**

**STAGE 3**

**STAGE 3** String a washer, the last nugget, and another washer on an eyepin. Use pliers or a one-step looper to make a simple loop at the other end of the pin (see page 22). Remove 1" (2.5cm) from the end of the small cable chain by opening a link with pliers, and attach it to one loop of the eyepin. Attach the rest of the small cable chain to the other loop.

**STAGE 4** Cut a strip of sari silk ribbon 4" (10cm) long, and wire wrap each end (see page 24).

**STAGE 5** Cut two pieces of sari silk ribbon 1" (2.5cm) long. Wire wrap the ribbons (see page 24) by pushing the long end of the wire through the center of both pieces and wrapping to form a little multilayered abstract flower charm.

STAGE 4

STAGE 5

**Tip Bead substitutions** If the frayed rustic ribbon isn't to your taste, substitute more chain, or more beads, and use a bought charm in place of the ribbon flower.

STAGE 6

**STAGE 6** Attach the wire-wrapped ribbon from Stage 4 to the short beaded strand with a jump ring.

The three strands that make up this bracelet don't have to be exactly the same length, but they should be similar. Remember that the strand with the big chunky beads will need to be a little longer so that the inside diameter will fit the wrist.

STAGE 7

**STAGE 7** Remove one ring from the large round chain—you may need to cut through the soldered join with diagonal wire cutters. With jump rings, attach one end of each strand to the single ring, and the other end to the remaining round chain.

STAGE 8

**STAGE 8** Attach the hook clasp to the single large ring. With the last jump ring, attach the ribbon flower charm to one of the links in the short section of small cable chain.

**Finished bracelet:**
7¹⁄₂" (19cm) long

## YOU WILL NEED

### BEAD BOX
- 62 labradorite 6-15mm chips (A)
- 124 copper 4mm triangular washers (B)
- 13 labradorite 12 x 7mm oblong pillows (C)
- 48 labradorite 8mm puff squares (D)
- 14 Czech glass 10mm matte metallic-coated faceted rounds (E)
- 9 labradorite 15 x 20 x 6mm briolettes (F)

### HARDWARE
- .018" (.46cm) flexible beading wire
- 6 copper 2 x 2mm crimp tubes
- 6 copper 4mm wire guardians
- 2 copper 8mm jump rings
- 2 copper 4mm jump rings
- 1 hammered brass 32 x 22mm two-part circular clasp (or clasp of your choice)

### TOOLKIT
- Diagonal wire cutters
- Bead stoppers or paper clips
- Flat-nosed pliers (2 pairs)
- Two-step crimping pliers

**Finished necklace:** Approximately 17" (43cm) long

# Rugged rocks necklace

The timeless appeal of this statement necklace lies in its balance between order and chaos. Irregular labradorite chips and briolette pendants are combined with more geometric shapes in a harmonious, formal design held together with chunky copper washers. Enjoy the contrast of rough and smooth textures and the unpredictability of the mysterious blue-green "flash" that lives deep within the stone.

**See it GROW**

## SHORT STRAND

**STAGE 1** Cut 17" (43cm) of beading wire and put a bead stopper or paper clip on one end. String [A, B, C, B, A, B, D, B] four times. String A, B, C, B, and A. At each end, string [B, C] ten times, followed by a final B. The strand should be approximately 14" (35.5cm) long.

**STAGE 1**

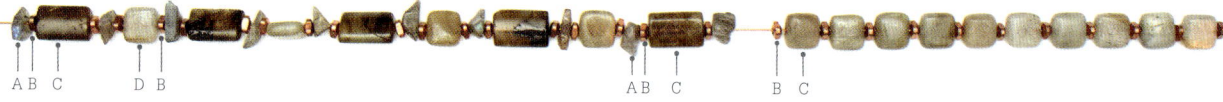

A B C    D B                         A B  C        B  C

STAGE 2

## MIDDLE STRAND

**STAGE 2** Cut 18" (45cm) of wire. String [B, two As, B, E] ten times, followed by B, two As, and B. At each end, string [C, B] ten times. The strand should be approximately 15" (38cm) long.

STAGE 3

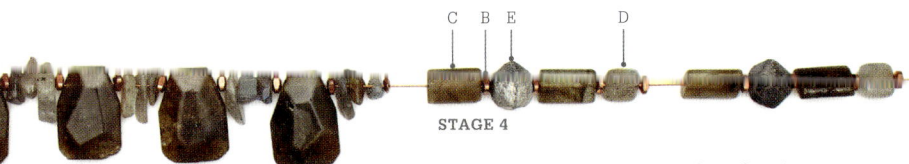

STAGE 4

## LONG STRAND

**STAGE 3** Cut 19" (48cm) of wire. String [B, three As, B, F] nine times, then B, three As, and B. Use the largest and chunkiest of your stone chips (A). If some of them have the hole near one end, so much the better.

**STAGE 4** At each end, string [C, B, E, B, C, B, D, B] twice. The strand should be approximately 16" (41cm) long.

STAGE 5

**STAGE 5** Finish each end of each strand with a crimp, a B washer, and a wire guardian. Pass back through the B, crimp, and another couple of beads.

**STAGE 6** Secure the crimps (see page 22) and trim the short ends of the wires.

**STAGE 7** Link the ends of the strands together using the 8mm jump rings (see page 23).

**STAGE 8** Use the 4mm jump rings to attach the clasp to the necklace ends.

### KNOW YOUR MATERIALS: LABRADORITE

Turn this understated semiprecious stone to the light and you'll see the blue, green, or rainbow "flash" that is the true beauty of this mineral. It's known as labradorescence, and is caused by tiny parallel layers within the stone. These reflect and break up visible light to give pure, bright colors that can only be seen from certain angles. The effect is sometimes enhanced by cutting facets into the stone.

Labradorite's neutral coloring means that it fits well into many different palettes and styles, and you'll find it in several projects in this book. It is widely available and relatively inexpensive. Quality is variable, but even the roughest, most irregular strand of labradorite chips can find a place in your designs. Just take care to remove any beads that are cracked, chipped, or sharp.

STAGE 7

STAGE 8

**Finished necklace:**
Approximately 18" (45cm) long

### ALTERNATIVE COLORS

The heart focal and the lentil beads used in this necklace are unique handmade items. Don't worry too much if you can't find exactly the same thing. Plenty of artisans make shanked heart buttons or pendants, and the 20mm lentil is a standard shape and size for lampwork beads. You can change the blue agate for a 6mm round bead of a different color to match your glass beads. The monochrome hematite and silver go with pretty much any color; the design principles and the stringing techniques in this project will still enable you to make a stunning necklace.

# True blue heart necklace

Hematite beads add sleek, sophisticated detail to a deceptively simple-looking necklace of handmade glass, crystal, agate, and silver. Learn how to string a shanked button as the focal point in this timelessly elegant design.

Clear red glass with carnelian

Mottled green and gray glass with malachite

**See it GROW**

**STAGE 1** Cut a 24" (60cm) length of wire and put a bead stopper on one end. String one A, three Bs, and one C, and the shank of the button. Repeat the bead stringing sequence in reverse.

A B C

A H G A E    F    E A    D

STAGE 1

STAGE 2

Check the button from the front. The silver rounds should be just visible beyond the edges. If they aren't, adjust the number of heishi at the back.

STAGE 3

STAGE 4

STAGE 5

**STAGE 2** String the following: D, A, E, F, E, A, the first hole of a G, H, the second hole of the G, and A.

**STAGE 3** Repeat the sequence shown in Stage 2 a further three times.

**STAGE 4** String D, A, the first hole of a G, H, the second hole of the G, and A. Repeat this sequence once more.

**STAGE 5** Transfer the bead stopper to the other end of the wire and repeat Stages 2–4 on the other side of the necklace. Check the length, allowing for the length of your chosen clasp plus approximately 1" (2.5cm), and add or subtract beads until you're happy.

## YOU WILL NEED

**BEAD BOX**
- 34 silver 2mm rounds (A)
- 10-16 hematite 3mm heishi disks (B)
- 2 hematite 4mm rounds (C)
- 25 x 20mm silver heart-shaped button with shank
- 14 hematite 8mm rounds (D)
- 16 black diamond 4mm Austrian crystal bicones (E)
- 8 blue and gray 20mm lampwork glass lentils (F)
- 12 hematite 10mm or 12mm rondelles with 7mm hole (G)
- 12 blue-dyed 6mm agate rounds (H)

**HARDWARE**
- .018" (.46mm) beading wire
- 2 silver 2 x 2mm crimp tubes
- 2 silver 4mm wire guardians
- 2 silver 4mm crimp covers
- 2 silver 6mm heavyweight jump rings
- 20mm silver hook clasp
- 4mm silver jump ring

**TOOLKIT**
- Diagonal wire cutters
- Bead stopper or paper clip
- Flat-nosed pliers (two pairs)
- Crimping pliers

**STAGE 6** Finish one end with D, B, a crimp tube, another B, and a wire guardian. Take the wire end back through the last few beads and secure the crimp with crimping pliers (see page 22).

**STAGE 7** Remove the bead stopper and finish the other end as for Stage 6. Leave a tiny bit more bare wire than you usually would, to allow for the crimp covers. Trim any spare ends of wire and use pliers to close a crimp cover carefully around each crimp. Open a 6mm jump ring (see page 23) and use it to attach the hook to one end of the necklace.

**STAGE 8** Use the 4mm jump ring to attach the other 6mm jump ring to the other end.

STAGE 6

STAGE 7

STAGE 8

## YOU WILL NEED

### BEAD BOX

- 5 gray speckled 10-15mm matte lampwork glass pebble beads
- 3 brown or green 15mm matte pressed glass ovals and/or rectangles
- 3 olive 14mm Picasso Czech table-cut glass flowers
- 6 assorted 8-10mm Celtic patterned pewter beads
- 6 gray 10mm pressed glass hearts and/or tulips
- 3 green 8mm garnet coin beads
- 3 olive 4 x 6mm jade faceted rondelles
- 6 gray 3 x 6mm matte glass heishi disks
- 6 olive 3 x 4mm pressed glass faceted rondelles
- 7-10 gray 4mm labradorite rounds
- 10 burgundy 4mm Austrian crystal bicones
- A few seed beads in toning colors–the mix shown here includes: 6º matte amethyst AB and matte metallic khaki iris; 8º silver; 11º chartreuse lined olivine AB
- A few orchid 8º matte triangle beads

### HARDWARE

- .018" (.46mm) flexible beading wire
- 6 silver 2 x 2mm crimp tubes
- 6 silver 4mm jump rings
- 3 silver toggle clasps (or clasps of your choice)

### TOOLKIT

- Diagonal wire cutters
- Bead board (optional)
- Bead stoppers or paper clips
- Flat-nosed pliers (2 pairs)
- Magical crimping pliers

**Finished bracelets:** Approximately 7¹⁄₂" (19cm) long; will combine into a necklace approximately 23" (58cm) long.

**Tip Random stringing** A challenge to many beaders, random stringing and its apparent lack of rules can be daunting, with messy and unbalanced results. However, this project will help you gain confidence in making a bunch of diverse beads work happily together.

# Highland heather bracelet

This threeway bracelet project has a Celtic feel. The muted hues of stone, cloud, moss, and heather combine with shining silver to make a set that can be worn in different ways: for example as stacking bracelets; a choker and bracelet set; or all together as a striking long necklace.

**STAGE 1**

**See it GROW**

**STAGE 1** Divide your beads into three roughly equal groups. Set aside a green glass rondelle and a gray glass heishi disk from each group.

**STAGE 2** Cut three lengths of wire, each approximately 10" (25cm) long. Put a bead stopper on one end of one length of cable. String a 8º silver seed bead and then the rest of one of your groups of beads. Remember to put seed beads in between the larger beads for flexibility. String 6½" (16cm) of beads (or your desired length allowing for the clasp). End with a 8º silver seed bead. Set this strand aside.

**STAGE 2**

**STAGE 3**

**Tip** **Bead variations** The bead box list is not set in stone. Start with some nice handmade lampwork beads and/or gemstones and build a palette around them. If you don't have exactly the same beads, simply substitute something of a similar size and the right sort of color.

**STAGE 3** Put a bead stopper on the next piece of wire and string the second group of beads, including a 8º silver seed bead on each end. Compare this strand to the first one as you go, so that the beads end up in a different order. String the same length of beads and set aside.

**STAGE 4** Repeat Stage 3 with the third piece of wire. You should have three strands of beadwork all the same length. Adjust the length with smaller beads if necessary.

**STAGE 5**

Alternate large and small feature beads when stringing, so the large beads are fairly evenly distributed along the length, and use rhythm and repetition to satisfy the eye. Don't be rigid, but do be at least a little consistent. For example, in these three bracelets, the lampwork beads always have crystals on either side, and wherever an olive jade rondelle is used, it is always next to a gray glass heishi disk.

**STAGE 5** Add a crimp and the set-aside gray heishi disk to one end of the first strand. Take the end of the wire back through the last few beads, leaving a small gap, and secure the crimp (see page 42). Do the same at the other end, adding the set-aside green rondelle after the crimp.

**STAGE 6** Crimp the other two strands in the same way. Use jump rings and flat-nosed pliers to attach a toggle clasp to each bracelet (see page 23).

**STAGE 6**

## YOU WILL NEED

### BEAD BOX

- 60 Austrian crystal 4mm bicones in at least five colors (fire opal, smoked topaz AB, jet, rose AB2x, padparadscha AB) (A)
- 36 copper 11º metal seed beads (B)
- 5 lampwork glass rounds approx. 15mm diameter (C)
- 20 transparent orchid 8º seed beads (D)
- 4 black 12mm lava rounds (E)
- 22 copper penny 4mm glass disk spacers (F)
- 20 8º matte black seed beads (G)
- 16 black 6mm lava rounds (H)

### HARDWARE

- 36 copper 1" (25mm) headpins
- .018" (.46mm) flexible beading wire
- 2 copper 2 x 2mm crimp tubes
- 2 copper 4mm wire guardians
- 2 copper 4mm jump rings
- 1 copper 12mm lobster claw clasp
- 1 copper 6mm jump ring

### TOOLKIT

- Round-nosed pliers
- Flat-nosed pliers
- Diagonal wire cutters
- Bead stopper or paper clip
- Two-step crimping pliers

**Finished necklace:** Approximately 18" (45cm)

# Volcanic vision necklace

Show off a beautiful set of handmade lampwork beads with a dramatic contrast between matte black lava stone and sparkling Austrian crystals. The overall formality of the design is tempered with a touch of playful randomness.

**See it GROW**

**STAGE 1** Choose 36 crystal As (five or six of each color). String one A and one B on a headpin, and make a wrapped-loop dangle (see page 24). Make a total of 36 dangles.

B →
A →

Wrapped-loop dangles x 36

C   A D  6 dangles  E  F G A

**STAGE 2**

You may find it helps to sort your wire-wrapped dangles into groups of six before stringing the necklace, so that the color distribution is approximately even. Or lay out your remaining crystals on a bead board and rearrange them until you're happy.

**STAGE 2** Cut a 20" (50cm) piece of flexible beading wire and put a bead stopper or paper clip on one end. Starting with the center bead, string [C, A, D, six dangles, E, F, G, A].

**STAGE 3** Repeat the previous sequence twice more, but on the second repeat use H in place of E. Alternate D and G, and pick A colors at random.

**STAGE 3**

Use H in place of E in the second repeat.

**STAGE 4** Now string [D, H, F, G, A].

D H  F G A

**STAGE 4**

**STAGE 5** Repeat the Stage 4 sequence a further five times.

**STAGE 6** Finish with [D, H, F, G, a crimp tube, F, and a wire guardian]. Pass the end of the wire back through the final few beads and use crimping pliers (see page 22) to secure.

**STAGE 6**

D H  F G I F  J

**STAGE 7**

**STAGE 7** Remove the bead stopper or paper clip and repeat the stringing sequence on the other side of the necklace, omitting the first (center) C. Snug the beads together and secure the second crimp (see page 22).

**STAGE 8** Trim both ends of the wire and use the 4mm jump rings (see page 23) to attach the lobster claw clasp to one end and the 6mm jump ring to the other.

**STAGE 8**

**Tip Work with what you have** The lampwork used in this project was made with a specially reactive silver-rich glass called "Ekho" to give the bright, almost opalescent colors with that hint of blue that goes so well with the rainbow-finish crystals. If you can't find beads with this exact glass, substitute others of similar size, and change the colors of your crystals and seed beads until you're happy with the combination.

**STAGE 1** Attach a pinch bail to the top of a crystal heart (see page 24).

**STAGE 2** Open a jump ring (see page 23) and use it to attach the bail to the center loop at the bottom of the 7-to-1 connector.

**STAGE 3** Cut a 6" (15cm) length of beading wire and put a bead stopper or paper clip on the end. String one A bead, a crimp, 21 B tubes, a crimp, and another A.

**STAGE 4** Go back through the final A bead, the crimp, and one tube. Pull until there is a $\frac{1}{32}$" (1mm) loop. Secure the crimp flat with the very tip of your flat-nosed pliers, then trim the short end of wire.

## YOU WILL NEED

**BEAD BOX**
- 2 light Siam 10mm crystal top-drilled hearts
- 22 black onyx 3mm round beads (A)
- 132 short "liquid silver" $\frac{3}{32}$" (2.38mm) heishi tube beads (B)
- 28 Siam 2.5mm crystal bicones (C)

**HARDWARE**
- 2 silver 7 x 4mm pinch bails
- 14 silver 4mm jump rings
- 2 silver 28 x 5mm 7-to-1 connector bars
- .010" (5lb test) Soft Touch flexible beading wire
- 12 silver 1.1 x 1mm micro crimp tubes
- 2 silver earwires with loops

**TOOLKIT**
- Flat-nosed pliers (2 pairs)
- Diagonal wire cutters
- Bead stoppers or paper clips

**Finished earrings:** Approximately 2" (5cm) long by 1½" (3.8cm) wide

# Dramatic dangle earrings

Shimmering semicircles of silver dangle and sparkle around brilliant crystal hearts in these bold yet delicate earrings. Using "liquid silver" tube beads is a clever way to add impact while saving weight. The use of fine beading wire and the tiniest of crimp beads requires all your stringing skills and patience, but the results are head-turning and well worth the effort!

**Tip Crimping in miniature**
Note that you need fine beading wire and micro crimps for this design, because ordinary beading wire and standard-sized crimps are too heavy and clumsy. You can't use your crimping pliers here because the wire is too fine, and there simply isn't space. Just squash the crimps with the tips of your flat-nosed pliers, as neatly as you can. The crimps are so small, nobody will even notice them!

Use a jump ring to connect each strand to the relevant loop on the connector bar.

**STAGE 5** Crimp the other end of the strand in the same way, ensuring there is a 1/32" (1mm) gap above the tube beads to allow the strand to curve. Use jump rings to attach the ends to the connector bar on either side of the heart.

**STAGE 6** Make another strand in the same way, using 27 B tubes and forming a 1/16" (2mm) loop at each end. Attach to the next loops on the connector bar.

**STAGE 7** For the final strand, string C, A, C, and a crimp. Then string [three Bs, C, A, C] six times, inserting a crimp after the final set of three Bs. Finish the ends and attach to the outermost loops of the connector bar.

**STAGE 8** Attach an earwire to the single loop of the connector. Make a second earring in the same way.

**Tip** **Alternative ideas** Try different crystal colors and shapes in the center, or play with the beads on the loops to produce different patterns. If you don't have "liquid silver" beads, try tiny metal seed beads instead. Add tiny drop beads, daggers, or top-drilled pendant bicones to the outermost loops for extra texture.

## YOU WILL NEED

### BEAD BOX
- 70 (approx.) brass 11° metal seed beads (A)
- 35 cherry red 6mm glass druks (B)
- 7 red Picasso 14 x 8mm glass twist ovals (C)
- 32 black 3mm onyx rounds (D)
- 4 orange Picasso 17 x 8mm table-cut glass navettes (E)
- 20 orange Picasso 5mm faceted pressed glass rondelles (F)
- 3 orange silver Picasso 12 x 14mm table-cut glass hearts (G)
- 1 red 20 x 30mm flattened lampwork focal bead
- 3 red and gray 14mm lampwork rounds

### HARDWARE
- 30 brass 2" (50mm) eyepins
- 1 brass finish 18mm magnetic ball clasp
- 7 brass 4mm jump rings
- 2 brass 8mm jump rings
- 8 brass 2" (50mm) headpins

### TOOLKIT
- One-step looper (or round-nosed pliers and diagonal wire cutters)
- Flat-nosed pliers (2 pairs)

**Finished necklace:** Approximately 18¹/₂" (47cm) long

# Glowing treasures necklace

A collection of little glass treasures displayed in a vibrant, asymmetric collage that's a whole lot of fun to put together. All you need are simple wirework skills and a bit of imagination... and plenty of beads!

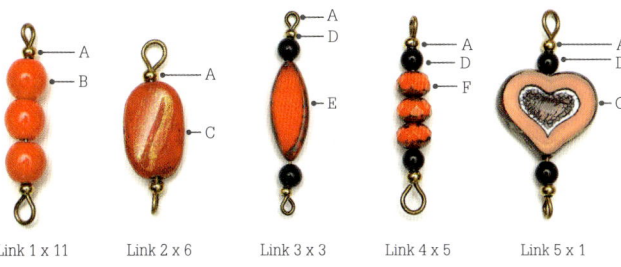

Link 1 x 11    Link 2 x 6    Link 3 x 3    Link 4 x 5    Link 5 x 1

On one of the links replace the D beads with F beads.

Magnetic clasp

STAGE 2

When making eyepin links for a chain, keep the loops at right angles. This helps your chain to hang and drape evenly when the links are connected, and gives a more professional finish.

**See it GROW**

## MAKING THE LINKS

**STAGE 1** On an eyepin, string an A bead, three B beads, and an A. Make a simple loop at the other end (see page 22). This is Link 1. Make 11 in total. Make four other types of link, as follows:
Link 2 [A, C, A], make six;
Link 3 [A, D, E, D, A], make three;
Link 4 [A, D, three Fs, D, A], make five;
and Link 5 [A, D, G, D, A], make just one.

**STAGE 2** Make four more eyepin links with the focal bead and lampwork rounds, stringing A, D, lampwork bead, D, A, except for one, where you replace the D beads with F beads. Using two pairs of pliers to open and close the loops (see page 23), connect the focal bead, the magnetic clasp, and two lampwork links.

Link 1      Link 2           Link 3

## THE BACK STRAND

**STAGE 3** Connect eight eyepin links in the following order: 1, 1, 2, 1, 1, 2, 1, 3. Attach the left-hand end to the second lampwork round above the clasp. Attach the right-hand end to the single lampwork link, using a 4mm jump ring to make the connection (see page 23). Attach an 8mm jump ring to the end loops of the chain.

STAGE 3

## THE INNER STRAND

**STAGE 4** Connect five eyepin links into a chain in the following order: 4, 4, 3, 4, 4.

## THE MIDDLE STRAND

**STAGE 5** Connect six more eyepin links into a chain in the following order: 1, 1, 2, 1, 1, 1.

Link 4          Link 3

STAGE 4

Link 1        Link 2

STAGE 5

Continued next page

## THE OUTER STRAND

**STAGE 6** Use 4mm jump rings to join the remaining eyepin links together in the following order: 4, 2, 1, 3, 2, 5, 2.

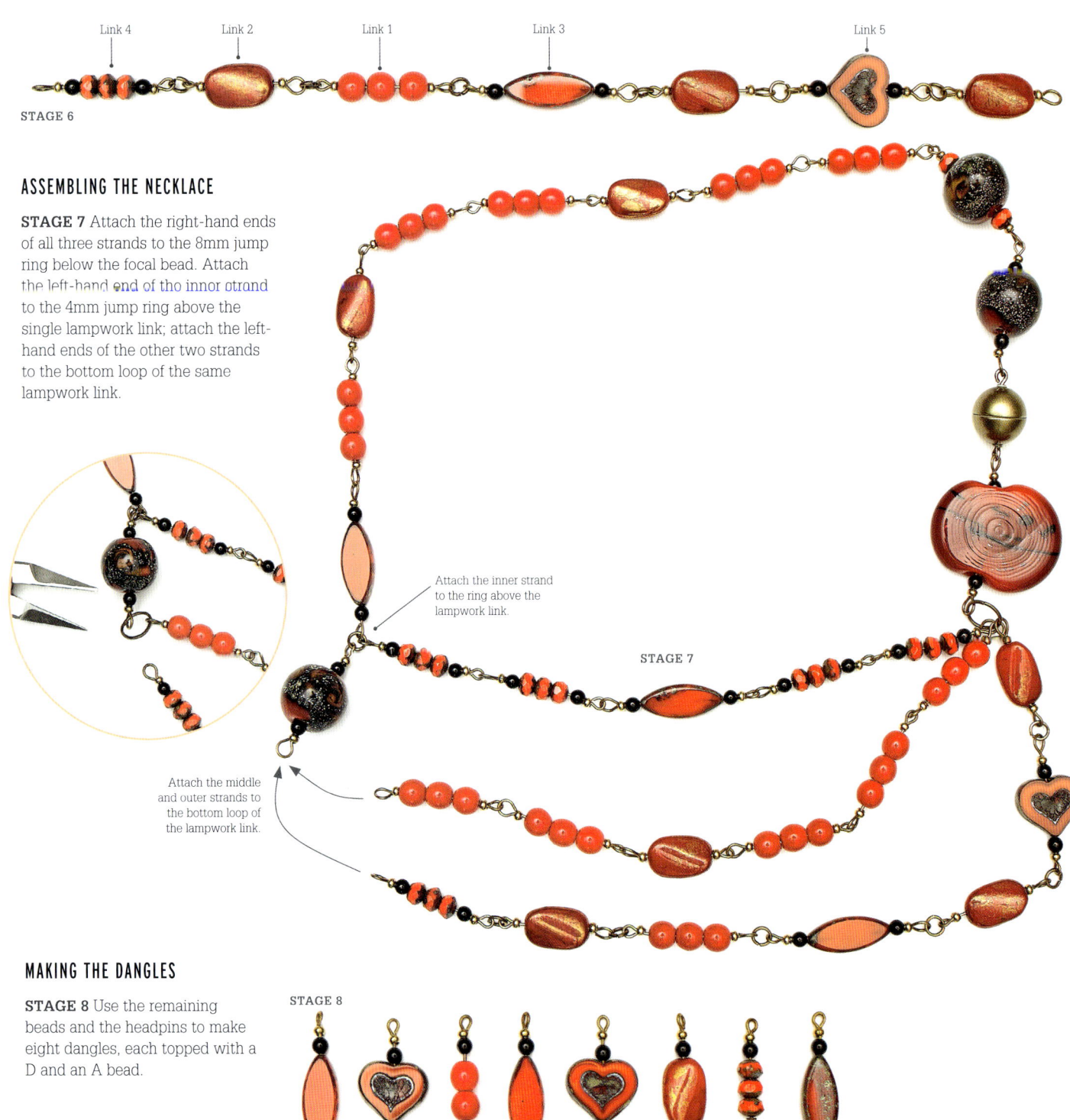

Link 4  Link 2  Link 1  Link 3  Link 5

STAGE 6

## ASSEMBLING THE NECKLACE

**STAGE 7** Attach the right-hand ends of all three strands to the 8mm jump ring below the focal bead. Attach the left-hand end of the inner strand to the 4mm jump ring above the single lampwork link; attach the left-hand ends of the other two strands to the bottom loop of the same lampwork link.

Attach the inner strand to the ring above the lampwork link.

STAGE 7

Attach the middle and outer strands to the bottom loop of the lampwork link.

## MAKING THE DANGLES

**STAGE 8** Use the remaining beads and the headpins to make eight dangles, each topped with a D and an A bead.

STAGE 8

**Tip Make and remake** Don't be worried by the asymmetric format. Give your subconscious free rein to assemble, arrange, and compose. The individual components are very easy to take apart and switch around until you're happy with how your necklace looks. And yes, you can use the same techniques to make a perfectly symmetrical composition (see page 17) if that's what you prefer. Just put the clasp at center back and make a more formal arrangement of links and dangles.

STAGE 9

Attach one headpin dangle to each of the jump rings, including the ring below the focal bead.

**STAGE 9** Attach one headpin dangle to each of the jump rings along the bottom of the necklace, including the 8mm jump rings at each end.

## KNOW YOUR MATERIALS: CZECH GLASS BEADS

Here are just a few pretty examples of Czech glass beads, many of which are still produced with antique equipment and traditional methods. There are numerous terms used to describe them:

**Pressed beads** are made by pressing hot glass between two halves of a mold.

**Picasso beads** have a thin, mottled coating applied to the outer surface. This may cover the entire bead, or may be partially removed.

**Table-cut beads** have been cut and polished to show the inner color of the glass.

**Two-hole beads** offer many stringing possibilities.

Have fun browsing your local bead store and see what tiny treasures you can discover!

Some Czech beads are even large enough to use as focals.

# Drama queen necklace

Make a dramatic entrance. Glittering with crystals, edged with spikes and daggers, this prima donna of a necklace makes a statement that can't be ignored. Assemble your materials and prepare to rule the world!

## YOU WILL NEED

### BEAD BOX

- 12 jet 2.5mm crystal bicones (A)
- 5 crystal copper 18mm graphic crystal beads
- 5 copper 6mm "stardust" rounds (B)
- 4 crystal red magma 10mm crystal top-drilled hearts
- 5 crystal red magma 12.5mm crystal ring beads
- 29 vitrail 4mm crystal bicones (C)
- 3 crystal red magma 17mm crystal wild hearts
- 40 matte black 11º seed beads (D)
- 48 jet matte 5 x 16mm pressed glass daggers (E)
- 108 copper crystal and/or light topaz 2.5mm crystal bicones (F)
- 8 copper crystal 6mm crystal bicones (G)
- 16 vitrail 6mm crystal bicones (H)
- 34 jet 4mm crystal bicones (J)
- 5g (approx.) matte black 8º seed beads (K)
- 4 garnet 6mm crystal bicones (L)
- 6 crystal silver night 12mm crystal double spike beads
- 10 crystal copper 6mm crystal faceted briolettes (M)

### HARDWARE

- 5 copper 2" (50mm) eyepins
- 7 copper 6mm jump rings
- 1 copper 1" (25mm) headpin
- .018" (.46mm) flexible beading wire
- 3 copper 18 x 10mm leaf-pattern pinch bails
- 6 copper 2 x 2mm crimp tubes
- 6 copper 4mm wire guardians
- 2 copper 3-to-1 connectors
- 8 copper 4mm jump rings
- 1 copper 25mm S-hook clasp

### TOOLKIT

- Round-nosed pliers
- Flat-nosed pliers (2 pairs)
- Diagonal wire cutters
- Bead stoppers or paper clips
- Magical crimping pliers

**Finished necklace:** Approximately 16" (40cm) long

**See it GROW**

**STAGE 1** String one A bead, a graphic crystal, and one B bead onto an eyepin. Make a wire-wrapped loop at the top (see page 24). Repeat with the remaining four eyepins.

Pendant 1    Pendant 2    Pendant 3

**STAGE 2** Open a 6mm jump ring (see page 23) and carefully feed it through the hole in each 10mm heart. Close the ring. Attach two of the rings directly to each of two eyepins. These are Pendant 1. Attach the others by means of another 6mm jump ring. These are Pendant 2. String one C bead, one hole of a ring bead (from inside to outside), and one A bead onto the headpin and make a simple loop (see page 23). Attach this dangle to a 6mm jump ring and the loop of the final eyepin. This is Pendant 3.

This pendant is at the center.

**STAGE 3** Cut approximately 20" (50cm) of beading wire. String [D, E, F, E, F, E, D, G, Pendant 1, and G]. Then string [D, A, E, F, E, F, E, A, D, H, Pendant 2, and H]. Finally, string [D, A, E, F, E, F, E, J, K, L, and Pendant 3]. Repeat the sequence in reverse.

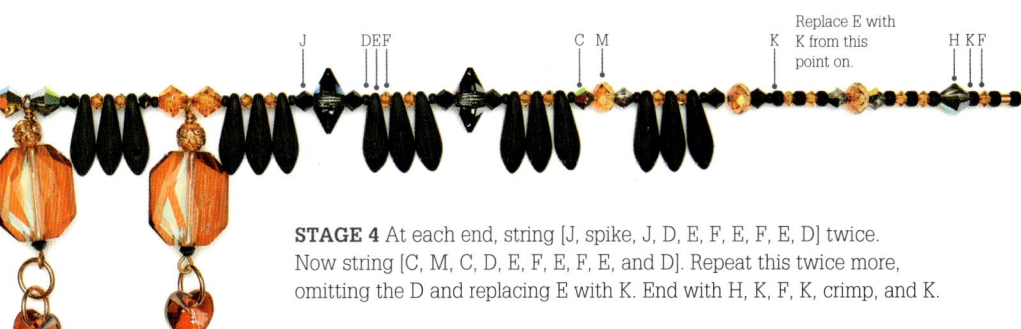

Replace E with K from this point on.

**STAGE 4** At each end, string [J, spike, J, D, E, F, E, F, E, D] twice. Now string [C, M, C, D, E, F, E, F, E, and D]. Repeat this twice more, omitting the D and replacing E with K. End with H, K, F, K, crimp, and K.

Continued next page

**STAGE 5** Attach the wild hearts to the pinch bails. Cut 18" (45cm) of wire. For the center part, string [D, E, F, E, F, E, J, D, G, wild heart, and G], then repeat twice, with L instead of G in the first repeat. String D, J, E, F, E, F, E, and D.

**STAGE 5**

DEF    JDG           L            DJ EF

**STAGE 6** At each end, string J, spike, J, and D. String [K, F, K, F, K, C, M, C, K, F, K, F, K, H] twice, then [K, F, K, F, K, C] three times. End with K, F, crimp, and K.

Replace E with K from this point on.

**STAGE 6**

JDK F    C M        H

**STAGE 7** For the center part, string [J, D, ring, C, other hole of ring, D, J, K, F, K, F, K] three times, then J, D, ring, C, other hole of ring, D, and J.

**STAGE 7**

J D    C    K F

**STAGE 8** At each end, string [K, F, K, F, K, H] four times, then [K, F, K, F, K, C] three times. End with K, F, K, crimp, and K.

**STAGE 8**

K F    H                           C              K F    K

**STAGE 9**

**STAGE 9** At each end of each strand in turn, pass the wire through a wire guardian and back through the last bead, the crimp, and a couple more beads. Secure the crimps (see page 42) and trim the short ends of the wires.

**STAGE 10** Use 4mm jump rings to attach all three strands of the necklace to the three-holed ends of the connectors. Make sure the strands don't cross.

**STAGE 10**

**STAGE 11** Use the remaining 4mm and 6mm jump rings to attach the "S" clasp to the other side of the connectors. Squash one side of the clasp closed so it can't fall off the ring. The other side should be opened just enough to allow the ring to pass in and out of the hook.

**Tip** **Pendant alignment** Note that the orientation of the loops on your eyepin dangles will change depending on whether you're hanging one jump ring or two underneath. For the pendants with one jump ring, the loops need to be at right angles; for pendants with two jump rings, the wrapped loop should be on the same plane as the loop of the eyepin. This ensures that all the pendants hang facing the front.

## YOU WILL NEED

**BEAD BOX**
- 4 hanks of 11º Czech seed beads: one hank each of light orange, dark orange, light red, and dark red
- 100 (approx.) clear AB 2mm Austrian crystal faceted rounds
- 2 silver 4mm rounds

**HARDWARE**
- White braided beading thread (PowerPro or Fireline 6lb test)
- 5 silver 6mm soldered jump rings
- E-6000 glue (optional)
- 2 silver 1" (25mm) eyepins
- 2 silver end cones
- 2 silver 6mm jump rings
- 1 silver 12mm lobster claw clasp

**TOOLKIT**
- Scissors
- Bead spinner
- Beading needle
- Diagonal wire cutters
- Round-nosed pliers
- Flat-nosed pliers

# Light my fire necklace

Sparkle and glow in this stunning necklace of fiery reds and oranges. The vibrant effect is achieved with only four different colors of seed beads, a sprinkling of crystals, and clever use of a bead spinner. You don't have to learn complicated beadweaving stitches to make something amazing with tiny beads!

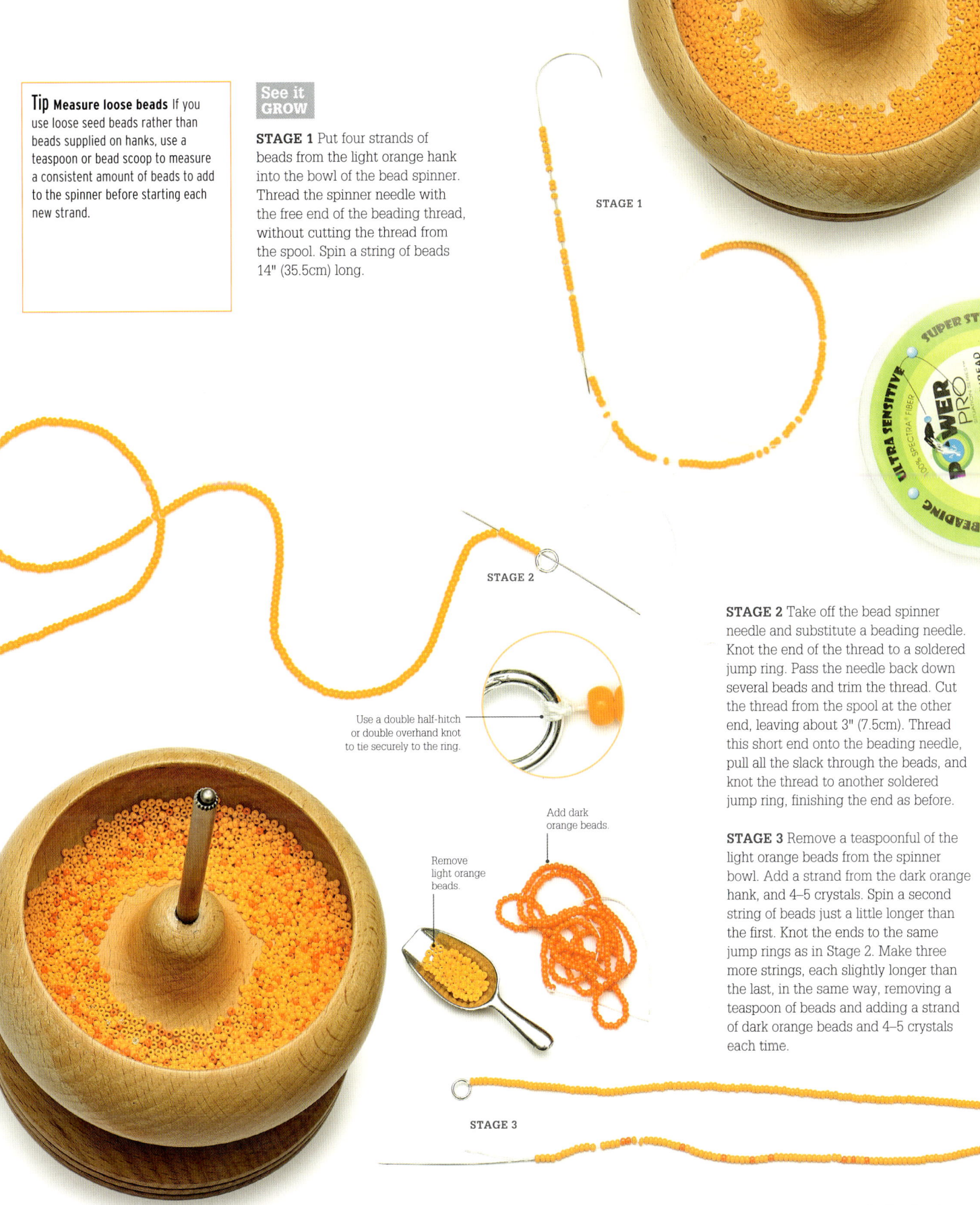

**See it GROW**

**Tip Measure loose beads** If you use loose seed beads rather than beads supplied on hanks, use a teaspoon or bead scoop to measure a consistent amount of beads to add to the spinner before starting each new strand.

**STAGE 1** Put four strands of beads from the light orange hank into the bowl of the bead spinner. Thread the spinner needle with the free end of the beading thread, without cutting the thread from the spool. Spin a string of beads 14" (35.5cm) long.

STAGE 1

STAGE 2

Use a double half-hitch or double overhand knot to tie securely to the ring.

Remove light orange beads.

Add dark orange beads.

**STAGE 2** Take off the bead spinner needle and substitute a beading needle. Knot the end of the thread to a soldered jump ring. Pass the needle back down several beads and trim the thread. Cut the thread from the spool at the other end, leaving about 3" (7.5cm). Thread this short end onto the beading needle, pull all the slack through the beads, and knot the thread to another soldered jump ring, finishing the end as before.

**STAGE 3** Remove a teaspoonful of the light orange beads from the spinner bowl. Add a strand from the dark orange hank, and 4–5 crystals. Spin a second string of beads just a little longer than the first. Knot the ends to the same jump rings as in Stage 2. Make three more strings, each slightly longer than the last, in the same way, removing a teaspoon of beads and adding a strand of dark orange beads and 4–5 crystals each time.

STAGE 3

Continued next page

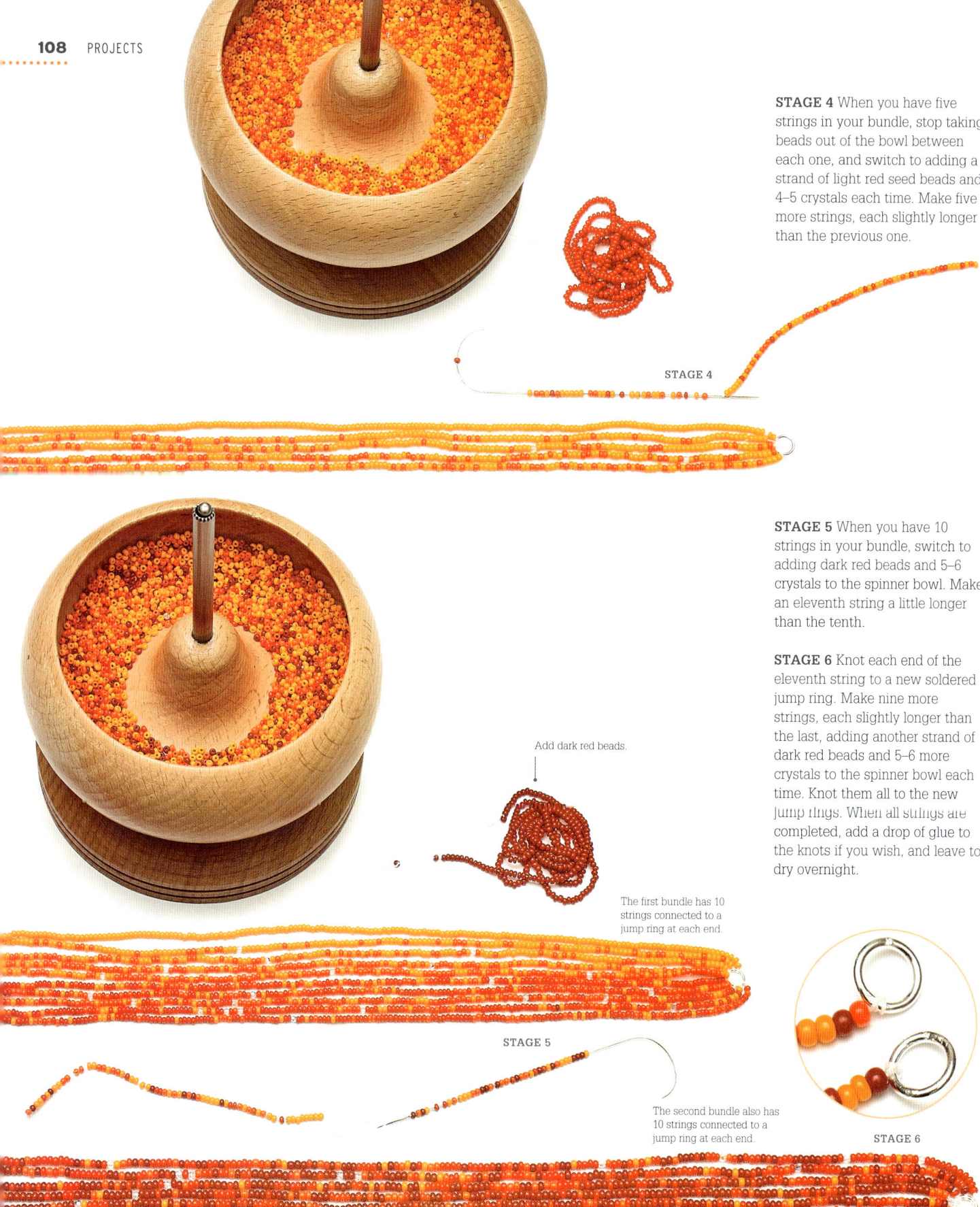

**STAGE 4** When you have five strings in your bundle, stop taking beads out of the bowl between each one, and switch to adding a strand of light red seed beads and 4–5 crystals each time. Make five more strings, each slightly longer than the previous one.

STAGE 4

**STAGE 5** When you have 10 strings in your bundle, switch to adding dark red beads and 5–6 crystals to the spinner bowl. Make an eleventh string a little longer than the tenth.

**STAGE 6** Knot each end of the eleventh string to a new soldered jump ring. Make nine more strings, each slightly longer than the last, adding another strand of dark red beads and 5–6 more crystals to the spinner bowl each time. Knot them all to the new jump rings. When all strings are completed, add a drop of glue to the knots if you wish, and leave to dry overnight.

Add dark red beads.

The first bundle has 10 strings connected to a jump ring at each end.

STAGE 5

The second bundle also has 10 strings connected to a jump ring at each end.

STAGE 6

**STAGE 7** Open the loop of an eyepin (see page 23) and connect it to the jump rings at one end of the first and second bundles of beaded strings. Do the same at the other end. String an end cone and a round bead on each eyepin.

Connect an eyepin to two jump rings.

STAGE 7

**STAGE 8** Make a wire-wrapped loop in each eyepin (see page 24) above the round bead. Use the two unsoldered jump rings to connect the lobster claw clasp to one loop and the remaining soldered jump ring to the other.

STAGE 8

**Tip** **What to do with "bead soup"**
You'll have some "bead soup" left over when you've made this necklace. Spin up some short strands for a bracelet, or use the beads for embroidery or collage projects. Or, why not use it as the starting point for another color exploration?

# Index

# Credits

The Land of Odds bead store generously provided beads and findings for many of the projects.

**Land of Odds—Be Dazzled Beads   www.landofodds.com**

The author thanks her husband for many, many cups of tea and great advice on how to write a book synopsis; also the editorial, design, and photography team at Quarto Publishing for their endless patience and expert support.

This book is dedicated to the memory of Pollie Jeffery, a brave, funny, and generous lady, without whom the beading world is a less colorful place.

Artisan beads and components were handmade by the following:

*Bead chart, pages 14-15:* row 1, column 1 Kathryn Greer, 4 Emma Ralph, 7 Sue Reynolds, 9 Tan Grey; row 2, column 8 Sandy Fulbrook; row 3, column 1 Tan Grey, 2 Sally Carver, 7 Sue Harris, 8 Nan Fry; row 4, column 1 Helen Wyatt, 5 Sue Reynolds, 8 Tan Grey; row 5, column 1 Helen Chalmers, 6 Leah Curtis

*Alternate projects, page 17:* lampwork beads, Tan Grey

*Simple pleasures earrings, page 28:* floral, Laney Mead; duo, Diane Turton

*Teardrop trio necklaces, page 34:* heart focal, Joanne Joyce

*Wave pendant, page 36:* project focal, Helen Wyatt; ribbon, Diane Turton; technique focal, Kathryn Greer; lentil beadcaps, George Harper; lentil focal, Marlene Minhas

*Beach love beads, page 38:* spacers, Tan Grey

*Strandline bracelet, page 44:* green spacers, Tan Grey

*Marigold bracelet, page 52:* clasp, Linda Newnham

*Sunny morning bracelet, page 56:* disks and spacers, Tan Grey

*Rustic romance bracelet, page 60:* heart, Karina Thornhill

*Oval pendant, page 66:* focal, Jeanette Fletcher; saucers, Kathryn Greer

*Lilac lariat, page 70:* hearts, Sue Harris

*Forest glade necklace, page 72:* project focal, Julia Hay; panel and technique focals, Sandy Fulbrook

*Pear tree bracelet, page 76:* bird, Sandy Fulbrook

*True blue heart necklace, page 90:* button, Rebecca Crabtree; project lentils, Sally Carver; panel lentils, (top) Billie Jean Little and (bottom) Vicki Honeywill

*Highland heather bracelet, page 92:* pebbles, Julia Hay

*Volcanic vision necklace, page 94:* rounds, Sue Reynolds

*Glowing treasures collar, page 98:* focal, Tan Grey; rounds, Jolene Wolfe